THE INNER GYM

A 30-Day Workout for Strengthening Happiness

Light Watkins

D0949111

FIRST EDITION

Cover design by Janina Brandão
Portrait by Danika Singfield

Watkins, Light

The Inner Gym: A 30-day Workout For Strengthening Happiness
Light Watkins—First edition.
ISBN 978-0-9908118-0-0

DEDICATED TO

*All of my teachers
and to those who inspired the
stories within this book*

THANK YOU TO MY EDITORS

Bruce Lilly, Lisa Gonzalez, Linnea Hunt-Stewart, and Vivian Delchamps

A special thanks to all of my Beta testers:
Torrey DeVitto, Everett Goldner, Donna Hansen,
Tiffany Baker, Dzee Louise, Tahlia Gray, Omar Ross,
Winston Scully, Arvo Zylo, Leonid Rozenberg, Kendy
Veazie, AE Gaupp, Jonathan Leaf, Melissa Ryan, Amy
Wohl, James Brown, Laura Hall, Matt Ushkow,
Boaz Reisman, Janean Mann, Emily Cavalier,
Kendra Walker, and Erica Berger

And to my family and friends who supported
and encouraged me to keep writing, namely
Bryndan Moore, Dhru Purohit, Antonio Neves,
Will Dalton, and my beloved teacher Thom Knoles

YOUR INNER WORKOUT PLAN

*It is difficult to find happiness within oneself,
but it is impossible to find it anywhere else.*

— Arthur Schopenhauer

PREFACE

One afternoon, while in between appointments, I decided to grab a bite at one of my favorite vegan restaurants in Beverly Hills, figuring I could use the downtime to craft a response to an email I had recently received from a client regarding money—my least favorite subject to discuss over email. As I was enjoying my meal, the waiter approached my table wearing a cautious grin. "Can I ask you a question?" he said.

"Sure," I replied, placing my fork down to give him my full attention.

"What do you do for a living?"

Before I could say anything, he continued, "I'm just asking because you seem so happy, and it made me wonder what kind of job you had."

"I teach people how to meditate," I replied.

"Of course you do," he said, with a toothy smile. "It's rare to meet someone who is so genuinely *happy*."

"Thank you for saying that," I responded, a little surprised by his compliment, "but this is a vegan restaurant, and aren't vegans typically pretty happy too?"

"Your happiness is different," he answered. "It seems so effortless."

While I've heard this comment from strangers before, what I couldn't help but find ironic about my waiter's observation was that I never once thought about *being* happy. In fact, I'd been preoccupied by the money email, and I didn't feel that there was anything especially joyous about our interaction, which mainly consisted of our greeting, and my ordering a dish.

Regardless, the waiter kept asserting that I was exuding this rare form of happiness, and he needed to understand its source. He began firing questions at me: "What kind of meditation did I teach?" "How did it work?" and "How long did I meditate for each day?"

Shortly after that exchange, I hosted what some would call a "spiritual" gathering where I led an open meditation, followed by a brief talk on consciousness. A young woman named Amber was in attendance along with about 20 others. She was invited by a mutual acquaintance and sat quietly in the back. Later that night, Amber sent me an email stating that she felt inspired to learn meditation from me. Her reason:

"There is such a peace within you. You're effortlessly happy, consistently, and for no apparent reason, and I would love to have that."

Her email, coupled with my interaction in the vegan restaurant a day earlier, triggered a flashback to the moment when I first met my meditation teacher in 2003. He also seemed effortlessly happy, and after only a few minutes in his presence, I was ready to drink the Kool-Aid, so to speak. In fact, my meditation teacher would've easily registered at a ten-out-of-ten on the "Happiness Scale."

A little backstory: I once had a friend who liked asking people where they would rank their happiness on a scale from zero to ten, with a zero being severely depressed, and a ten being as happy as they could imagine feeling. The number they chose defined their "baseline level of happiness," and thus the answer to his question. According to my friend, most people's answers fell between a six and an eight.

Once the baseline level of happiness was determined (assuming they weren't at a ten) his next question was, "What would it take to get you to a ten?"

I've asked people this question before as well, and the most common answer I've received has been some variation of, "If only I had more money..."

What's interesting about that answer is how, according to extensive research on happiness, once our basic necessities are provided for, having more money does surprisingly little to increase it. In some instances, having more money can decrease our level of happiness!

In practical terms, if it were true that more money led to greater happiness, all of the wealthiest people on the planet would rate themselves at a permanent ten-out-of-ten on the happiness scale. The Mark Zuckerbergs, Warren Buffets, and Oprah Winfreys of the world would be happy 100% of the time. Obviously, this is not the case.

According to the *2013 World Happiness Report*, the United States of America, despite its unprecedented number of millionaires, billionaires and tech leaders, ranks only 17th on the list of the happiest nations.[i] The citizens of Iceland, Costa Rica and Panama (all countries with less wealth per capita) describe themselves as being happier, particularly when factoring in variables such as social support, perception of corruption, life expectancy, freedom to make life choices, and generosity. In fact, while the size of America's gross domestic product (GDP) has increased since 2007, individual levels of happiness have been on a steady decline.

I remember reading about a Dr. Carl Jung interview where he expressed his take on the correlation between wealth and happiness. Dr. Jung worked as a prominent psychiatrist all over the world for more than 50 years, and in the interview, the journalist asked Dr. Jung the following hypothetical question: if he could choose between working exclusively with wealthy patients or poor patients, which would he prefer? Without much hesitation, Dr. Jung said he'd choose the wealthy. This of course shocked the journalist into asking, "Why not the poor?" His answer: wealthy people often have the same problems as poor people, except they don't waste my time thinking the solution lies in having *more* money.

Jung was not suggesting that there was something inherently wrong with making money, improving our circumstances, accomplishing goals, or seeking out adventure and fun. He was just affirming what modern-day happiness studies have concluded: there is little correlation between achieving wealth and being a self-described "happy" person.

The initial wave of happiness we feel as a result of accomplishing our goals or finding material success favors the trajectory of your average two-dollar temporary tattoo—it's vibrant in the beginning, but faded after a few days. If Dr. Jung and the World Happiness Report are right, and the answer to becoming happier does not lie in acquiring more wealth, then where exactly is the source of our happiness?

The path to happiness was outlined in no uncertain terms 2,500 years ago by the Buddha, who supposedly said, "There is no *way* to happiness. Happiness *is* the way." In other words, happiness is not and has never been the by-product of acquisitions, but a lively state of consciousness that, once accessed, allows us to feel happy inside, and often for no particular reason.

While this advice rings true deep within our core, we may still wrestle with it because our cultural indoctrination takes the opposing view. Advertisements, songs, and movies teach us that happiness is *not* the starting point, but the end result of achieving material success, and finding true love; if we're not happy, it's likely because we haven't met the right person, bought the right item or had the right experience. This thinking is deeply ingrained into the psyche of every Western teenager approaching adulthood: if you fall in love with the right person, or get the right job, or come up with the million-dollar idea, or sell your company, you'll live happily ever after. The Buddha counters this logic by suggesting that you may be happy for a little while, but eventually you'll feel the same way you felt before your big achievement.

For argument's sake, let us suppose we side with the Buddha, and adopt the belief that there is no way to happiness—that happiness itself is the way. The question then becomes, if happiness is the way and not the end goal, how is it possible to *be* happy? If I'm clinically depressed, or if I owe more money than I make, if my spouse cheats on me, if I lose someone close to me, or if all of the above is happening to me at once, how can I be happy?

"You need to choose to be happy," a good friend or trusted confidant may advise you, as if choosing happiness over misery, anger, or fear is as simple as choosing to wear a blue shirt instead of a yellow one. Secondly, if it is that easy to choose to be happy, then why are fewer people in America choosing it each year? If happiness was just a choice away, why would anxiety disorders, including depression, count for a whopping one-fifth of all mental disabilities?[ii] My theory—the one that prompted me to title this book *The Inner Gym*—is that being happy is actually *less* of a choice and more like doing a pull-up.

We are what we repeatedly do.
Excellence, then, is not an act, but a habit.

— Aristotle

WARM UP

Being able to do a pull-up is largely dependent not on choice, but on physical strength. What if feeling happy inside was dependent not on choice, but on *emotional* strength? If true, then telling someone to override feelings of depression or anxiety and "choose to be happy" would be akin to telling someone who has never exercised before to overlook their muscle weakness and choose to do ten pull-ups.

The physically weak person will understandably view the task of doing ten pull-ups as frustrating and most likely impossible. It's not that he lacks the potential, the will, or the understanding of how to do a pull-up. He simply isn't strong enough for his will to match the demand of doing ten pull-ups.

However, someone else who has been training regularly will be better prepared to meet that same demand successfully, no matter when or where it is placed on her. The main difference is that one person invested the time to develop the required amount of physical strength to meet the demand, and the other person did not. Inner muscles work similarly.

By "inner muscles," I'm not referring to physical muscles, but to those internal forces that provide you with the strength and dexterity to successfully meet your emotional demands while preserving your inherent optimism, positivity and happiness.

An emotional demand could be any of the following:

- *Moving on after a relationship ends abruptly*
- *Having a difficult conversation*
- *Feeling rejected, disrespected or unappreciated*
- *Losing a close friend or relative*
- *Being verbally attacked*

Meeting any of these demands affects us emotionally, no matter how well-adjusted we are. They would significantly draw down on anyone's happiness levels—at least initially. For instance, it is doubtful that the average person would feel happy immediately after being verbally attacked or taunted by a loved one. But after some time passes (studies say emotions typically don't last longer than about 90 seconds)[iii], the distressful feelings should taper off. If, on the other hand, those negative feelings linger for several days, weeks, or even years after the incident, it is likely a sign of weak inner muscles.

Not being able to successfully adapt to emotional demands that are extremely commonplace in daily life can feel crippling, and lead to emotional instability. Let's look at some of the common symptoms of long-term emotional imbalance:

- *You often feel the need to recount negative experiences from your past*
- *You are easily triggered into feeling anxious*

- *Your mind runs a seemingly endless series of negative thought-patterns*
- *You frequently think of harming yourself or others*
- *You tend to be pessimistic most of the time*
- *You are often reactive, confrontational, argumentative or disagreeable*
- *You have low self esteem*
- *You feel depressed*
- *It is difficult for you to sleep or even just relax without medication, causing you to feel on edge*

We don't usually associate the above symptoms with happy people. It's not to say that people who display these symptoms are incapable of being happy, or that happy people never have these feelings. But there are ways to better understand how to "work out" our inner muscles, which can lead to greater emotional balance, even for those with severe or inherited chemical imbalances (*Disclaimer: the suggestions presented in this book are not meant to replace doctor-prescribed medical treatment for chemical imbalances*).

People with weak inner muscles may be happy some of the time, but their happiness is temporal, and linked to favorable external circumstances, such as getting a bonus at work. Unfavorable changes in external circumstances often lead to dramatic fluctuations in mood, or desperate attempts to control one's environment. In addition, one may feel unsubstantiated fear, sadness, anger or boredom.

Conversely, happy people with strong inner muscles can experience the inevitable losses and rejections of daily life and still find an easier time meeting those demands successfully. For them, happiness is not a choice that they must consciously make in difficult times; it is a state of awareness that they experience within themselves. Here are common symptoms of operating from an inner state of happiness, as a result of having strong inner muscles:

- *Your natural inclination is to see the best in others*
- *You smile easily and don't take yourself too seriously*
- *You feel a genuine sense of present moment awareness*
- *Your thoughts are mostly creative, positive and optimistic*
- *You often think of helping others before helping yourself*
- *You tend to be more empathetic, compassionate and caring*
- *You feel happy most of the time (in spite of your external circumstances)*
- *You fall asleep easily and feel rested upon awakening*

The idea of the inner gym is to condition you to feel effortlessly happy, despite your ever-changing external circumstances or your temporary emotional states.

To give it a little more practical context, let's say that you discover unexpected traffic on your way to an important job interview, and having to adapt to this change of expectation is the emotional equivalent of doing ten military-style push-ups in under a minute. Many people would find that demand challenging, but not impossible.

But what if the demand was bigger? Let's suppose that you were in a passionate three-year love affair that ended abruptly because your lover met someone else. To successfully adapt to this much larger emotional demand would be the equivalent of having to do 900 push-ups within five hours. What would it take for you (or anyone) to meet a physical demand of that severity? Wouldn't it heavily depend on the condition of your physical strength? Completing 900 push-ups within five hours is an average of three push-ups a minute for 300 straight minutes. If you've been training, it's certainly possible. If not, you may pass out from exhaustion after a couple of hours.

To take this example further, what if, after five hours, you don't finish all 900 push-ups and a new demand of 500 squats within three hours is placed on you. And after that, another demand of 500 pull-ups within four hours was coming? You may feel paralyzed by the very thought of having to perform so many exercises in such a short amount of time. Again, for someone who trains regularly, these are not unreasonably difficult physical goals, even when stacked on top of one another. Sure, they will be tough, but they are not impossible.

As life stacks one emotional demand on top of another, we may find ourselves feeling increasingly overwhelmed. Seldom does life wait until we meet one demand successfully before placing another one on us, and then another one, and another. Without training, we won't be able to keep up, and if we can't keep up, the only natural outcome is to become emotionally exhausted, unstable, or paralyzed.

Strengthening our inner muscles by working out in the Inner Gym is the equivalent to regularly practicing our push-ups, our squats, and our pull-ups so that we are ready for anything. If we want to feel happy and optimistic most of the time, we need to strengthen those inner muscles that are responsible for keeping us supremely adaptable to change. In an ever-changing world, one of our biggest assets as humans is our ability to adapt.

The less we are able to adapt, the more self-induced suffering we tend to experience, and the more we have to rely on choosing to be happy. On the other hand, the more we can adapt, the less suffering we experience and the happier we can become naturally, without having to choose it or even think about it much.

How To Use This Book

The purpose of this foundational phase of *The Inner Gym* is to familiarize you with your inner muscles—the ones directly responsible for happiness—and to provide you with a basic workout plan for exercising and strengthening those muscles so your happiness effortlessly shines through you. With strong inner muscles, you will have a far easier time allowing happiness to *be* the way in the moment, as the Buddha suggested, rather than waiting for it to come in the future.

This book is intended to be a quick read. In-depth explanations of the psychological reasons for unhappiness have purposefully been kept to a minimum. Some yogic and spiritual terms also lack depth and explanation. Instead of making this an intellectual pursuit, I want to encourage the reader to allow the answers to come from the inner workouts themselves.

The six inner exercises presented in this book are not new. They are all common practices taught throughout time by parents, grandparents, mentors, clergy, and friends. They are simple to execute and require only a few minutes each day. What you're getting with this book is exactly what makes the aforementioned physical exercises effective—you're getting a plan. You're also getting structure, sequence and accountability for building the strength of your inner muscles efficiently.

This program conditions you from the inside out. Inner workouts take place in real-life situations, where the incremental changes in your relationships and worldview will determine whether you're exercising correctly. Progress will be measured by assessing your baseline level of happiness, which you will monitor daily.

If your experience is anything like mine, the time you invest in these next 30 days will get refunded back to you in the form of better sleep, a stronger immune system, and the ability to make better life choices. As you grow to appreciate your inner muscles and depend on them to get you through challenging times, you'll quickly see that your outer strength pales in comparison to the potential you've carried inside of you all along, especially when it comes to being happy and staying happy.

Each chapter of The Inner Gym contains a short story illustrating the inner exercise you'll be practicing for five days, some background information about why you're performing the inner exercise, and detailed instructions on how to easily integrate the inner exercise into your life. You'll find an inner exercise log at the end of each chapter for you to record your results and track your progress (what you measure, you can improve). I've tried to keep the chapters short and concise enough to read in one sitting.

The Inner Gym is a practice-oriented program. It's designed to be done anywhere, and meant to be integrated into a busy life. So don't wait to start. For best results, it's also important not to skip ahead and start the next inner exercise before completing your five days of practice with the current inner exercise. However, if life gets busy, feel free to stay on any one of the inner exercises for longer, and enjoy the journey.

Are you ready to hit The Inner Gym?

Use the Force, Luke. Let go, Luke.

— Obi Wan Kenobi in *Star Wars*

INNER EXERCISE 1

BE STILL

(Days 1 to 5)

For those unfamiliar with *Star Wars*, the 1977 movie was a tale about Luke Skywalker rising from obscurity to defend the galaxy against Darth Vader and the evil empire. Created by George Lucas, *Star Wars* became the first summer blockbuster movie in history, and like many children of the 1970s, I was obsessed with pretty much everything about it.

"Use the Force" was the famous directive given to Luke from his Jedi teacher, Obi Wan Kenobi. The Force yielded supernatural powers to all of those who could harness it. Although there are multiple references to "the Force" echoed throughout the film, it remained an abstract concept even for Luke, who had to undergo very focused training to access it.

As Obi Wan described it, "the Force is what gives a Jedi his power. It's an energy field created by all living things. It surrounds us and penetrates us. It binds the galaxy together."

I spent countless hours channeling the Force through the use of my childhood imagination. As I grew into adulthood, my fascination with the Force was replaced by an obsession with yoga and Eastern spiritual practices.

I discovered yoga by accident in my mid 20's. While working out in a gym on the Upper West Side of Manhattan one evening, I noticed a gathering of young attractive women outside of the group exercise room. As they started filing in, something told me to follow behind, and before I knew it, I was taking my first yoga class. Despite my less-than-noble intentions, the practice stuck, and over the next few years I completely immersed myself into yoga.

I loved reading about the metaphysical nature of reality, especially stories about the gurus and yogis of ancient India, who were like the Jedi Knights of their day. Instead of wielding light sabers, they armed themselves with sacred knowledge and broadband access to deep states of consciousness.

I met a real-life guru—my own version of Obi Wan Kenobi—when I relocated from New York to Los Angeles a few years later. I was invited to a meditation talk at my yoga teacher's apartment. Although I was keenly interested in yoga, I wasn't necessarily searching for a meditation practice or teacher because I concluded in New York that my body was too stiff for meditating. To me, meditation was synonymous with torture. I dreaded it.

But I came to the talk anyway, mostly out of curiosity. I admired my yoga teacher and the way he moved through the world, and he had spoken so highly of his meditation teacher. There were about 30 of us from his yoga class packed into the living room, waiting for his teacher to arrive.

He told us to close our eyes, and while we sat in silence the teacher evidently snuck in from the back and tip-toed his way through the crowd, because the next thing I heard was, "You may now open your eyes." And settling into my friend's wooden armchair at the front of the room was not the old, bearded monk of my imagination, but a radiant, clean-shaven American man in his mid-50's. His tanned, boyish face exuded youthfulness and vibrancy. Instead of wearing a robe, he was garbed in business-casual attire—khaki slacks, a powder blue dress shirt and a hound's-tooth blazer. He easily contorted his legs into full lotus (a yoga posture with his legs crossed so deeply that the top of his bare feet rested on his opposite thighs).

Then came the introduction: "My name is Thom Knoles. I'm a meditation teacher with more than 30 years of experience and ten thousand students throughout the world."

He then smiled at us with his sapphire blue eyes followed by a soft chuckle, as if enjoying a silent, but very funny joke with himself. Next, he picked up his glass of water from the table and, holding it in front for everyone to see, tapped his golden tri-band pinkie ring against the side of the glass three times.

"Although you clearly heard the sound of my ring tapping this glass," he said, pausing to take a sip, "from a quantum physics perspective, nothing actually touched."

Thom began to elaborate on how everything we see, smell, taste, feel, and hear contains both particles and waves, and how they all emerge from a unified field that is made of pure consciousness. "This field creates, conceives, constructs, governs, and becomes each one of us," he said, striking a familiar chord with the Star Wars description of the Force.

"Meditation is the inner experience of merging back into that pure consciousness state," he explained, referring to the process nonchalantly as "transcending," as if he'd personally transcended thousands of times and it was no big deal.

"When your mind moves from surface thoughts back into pure awareness in meditation, time speeds up dramatically, your mind can effortlessly stop thinking, and your body will acquire the deepest rest possible, even deeper than sleep. It's an art as well as a science," he said.

Thom also referred to meditation as a practice originally intended for householders—regular people— and not just monks. He told us there were well-known styles of meditating that regular folks could use for accessing the deepest states of transcendence without much effort.

Thom spoke like a master, with just the right combination of humor and authority. I don't remember him ever using any fillers such as "um" or "ah," and I'd never heard anyone explain the inner workings of meditation with such elegance. He provided detailed scientific evidence and avoided the stock airy-fairy language you'd expect to hear at a talk on meditation.

"Meditation is not belief-based," he claimed, "nor is it faith-based. I can show you how to have your own direct experiences of transcendence and verify everything I'm talking about for yourself."

At the end of his captivating lecture, Thom told us that in order to properly learn how to meditate we must be initiated into his tradition, as he had been by his teacher, the Indian guru Maharishi Mahesh Yogi, decades before. His instructions were to return the next morning with two pieces of fruit, a handful of flowers, a new white cloth, and a financial contribution of a week's salary.

The first three would be used as offerings to his ancient Indian lineage, he said, motioning toward a photograph of a stern-looking, elderly Indian man with long hair and a gray beard. The photo was framed in dark wood, and propped against a vase of flowers on the table next to him. The man in the photo appeared to be sitting on a type of throne, while wearing an orange robe, with something white smeared across his forehead. Thom introduced him as his teacher's teacher, Swami something or another (I couldn't make out the tongue-twisting pronunciation, but it sounded important). He explained that the photograph was a representation of all of the teachers from his tradition dating back thousands of years.

The contribution of a week's pay would cover the cost of receiving personal instruction from Thom, plus pre-pay him for his time in case we ever needed to reach out with questions once the course was over, something he assured us would happen. I especially found this part of the arrangement intriguing. I never heard of someone charging so much for meditation instruction. But it got my attention, and I loved the idea of making a meaningful exchange of something I valued (my money) for something of greater value (his knowledge).

The only challenge was I didn't have steady income. But in my heart, the proposition of learning to meditate from someone like Thom, who was perhaps the smartest and happiest person I'd ever met, felt like a godsend, as if I stumbled upon an opportunity to buy pure gold for one penny on the dollar. So I scraped together $400 dollars in cash and showed up the next morning with my fruit and flowers. Thom took my offerings and performed a brief ceremony in Sanskrit, initiating me into his tradition. He then took me aside and whispered my mantra into my ear. Next, he showed us all how to sit comfortably with our eyes closed and softly repeat our mantras.

Over the next few days of the training, he instructed us to meditate with our personalized mantra twice a day for twenty minutes per sitting. In time and with consistency, he predicted that we would eventually lose awareness of our mantra and our minds would begin effortlessly falling silent in meditation.

Although Thom seemed sincere and confident, I was skeptical. In my past, having a tangible experience of inner stillness through meditation eluded me, no matter how much I tried, mantra or no mantra. Reading my mind, Thom told us not to try to go deep in meditation, nor to rely on what he said was supposed to happen in meditation. Instead, he advised us to follow the basic instructions and trust our own direct experiences.

I began meditating daily, as instructed. While the experience was relaxing, there was certainly no feeling of a consistently quiet mind. But one morning, about a month into my practice, I was meditating on my couch and began to sense something different from my ordinary thought-filled meditations. It started subtly, and slowly grew into an all-encompassing feeling of inner serenity. It was like being in a swimming pool that was filling up with pure energy. My thoughts began to subside; the gaps in between my thoughts grew wider. A moment later, I dropped into a void where there were no more thoughts of any kind, or bodily sensations. Everything just faded away. It's not that I disappeared or astral-travelled. It felt more like I became one with everything, sort of like the *Alice in Wonderland* line about forever lasting one second.

What startled me was emerging from this state after what seemed like five minutes and realizing that half an hour had flown by. Yet, I wasn't asleep and I was still sitting upright.

I recalled how Thom said this would happen when I *least* expected it, and that I should never look for it. He was right. I dabbled in meditation for a year or so prior to meditating in this way, and I never once had an experience even close to this.

Strangely, my next thought was about *Star Wars*, as it dawned on me that I'd just tapped into Obi-Wan's description of the Force, *"an energy field that surrounds us, penetrates us and binds the world together."* I then wondered if George Lucas ever meditated or knew that this state of awareness actually existed, and whether his experience with meditation was the inspiration for the concept of the Force.

I didn't reach the transcendent state again for a few meditations, probably because I started anticipating it. But when it eventually reoccurred, I marveled at how palpable and unique a feeling it was. Now meditation was exciting, and I couldn't wait to do it every day. After a few more months, the Force-like feeling became more prevalent, and began making guest appearances outside of my meditations too. I noticed various "superpowers," as my emotional reflexes improved. Sadness no longer had the same grip over me. I also found it easier to see the kernels of wisdom in otherwise challenging life situations. I could detect an innate connection between myself and others. Nature seemed to come alive and support me in magical ways.

Interestingly, I found my new state of awareness in the same place Obi Wan directed Luke Skywalker to access the Force—right at the point of letting go. In other words, I had to let go of my need for constant activity in order to journey beyond the ridge of my everyday mental clutter. Once there, the ocean of pure consciousness was patiently awaiting my discovery.

Having this experience gave me immeasurable benefits that ultimately led to clearer perception and more refined intuition, increased happiness, more rest, and even a stronger immune system.

Within my first few years of daily meditating, I realized that I'm not the only one who can access this state. Each of us has the potential for directly experiencing the unbounded ocean of consciousness that lies beyond our surface awareness, if only we would make the time. The reason I hadn't stumbled upon this deeper state prior to meeting my teacher was because I wasn't willing to give anything up. I wasn't going to wake up earlier, watch less television, or work less in order to sit with my eyes closed and do what I initially assumed was a waste of time. My attitude about inner work closely mirrored Luke Skywalker's when he first heard about the Force:

"Look, I can't get involved. I've got work to do. It's not that I like the Empire. I hate it, but there's nothing I can do about it right now.... It's all such a long way from here."

Translation: It sounds interesting, but it has no practical value for me, and therefore isn't worth my time or attention.

Luke felt it was more prudent to stay on his farm and attend to his daily affairs. Of course, this is the setup to one of the greatest adventure films in history. Likewise, your first inner exercise—to make a little time for daily meditation—could be the setup to *your* greatest adventure, as the key to true happiness has been within you all along. The more frequently you tap into it, the happier you will begin to feel, and the less you will have to rely on choosing to be happy, or looking for sustained happiness on the yonder side of acquisitions.

WHY MEDITATION?

When many people hear the word meditation, they immediately conjure up images of hippies, granola, discomfort, gong sounds, incense, and candles. Some people even put meditation in the same category as religion, or associate it with monasticism or ideas of detaching from the world. They incorrectly assume that in order to meditate successfully, they would have to give up coffee, alcohol, or meat.

Most others agree that meditation would be good for them, if only they didn't have such a busy mind, or an antsy body, or if only they had more spare time on their hands. It's a big misconception to think that you need a quiet mind in order to meditate effectively.

What if you didn't have to control your mind or body at all? What if there was a comfortable way to meditate, that didn't require you to sit on the floor in lotus pose, or keep your back straight? What if by being more comfortable and relaxed, meditation felt less like assembling IKEA furniture and more like a well-deserved tropical vacation? What if meditating refunded you back the time you didn't think you had, to do more of the things in life that you enjoy?

To begin, we need to examine all of the practical ways in which daily meditation passes the "so what?" test. Translation: how does making the time to meditate add real-world value to your life?

Daily life makes us all susceptible to accumulating stress, mostly due to the non-stop demands and pressures of juggling work, home and personal responsibilities. This stress revs up the nervous system, causing the brain to flood the body with hormones that trigger overreacting, irrational thinking, and even insomnia. After years of unavoidable exposure to the stress reaction with no defense, the nervous system can become severely deteriorated, leaving us defenseless against mental or physical illness and disease.[iv]

As it happens, meditation has been proven as one of the greatest counter-stress solutions.[v] When practiced daily, meditation can help to restore balance and re-supply much-needed rest to your physiology. Common side effects of daily meditation are increased energy and feelings of contentedness and inner happiness.[vi]

Meditating daily will not only repair your body from the long-term effects of stress, but it has also been scientifically proven to enhance brain power, which will allow you to achieve a level of clarity never before experienced. You will notice more refined intuition and have an easier time honing in on the "bigger picture" aspects of your life circumstances.

Over these next five days, you're going to explore the practice of daily meditation, and use it to give your mind and body much needed outlets for the release of stress. This is a key habit that you will form over these next 30 days and beyond. In fact, your entire Inner Gym workout hinges upon your commitment to meditating for just five to ten minutes each day.

Perhaps you either already meditate, or you could easily sit for much longer than five to ten minutes. That's great, and as you begin to experience the benefits of a consistent meditation practice, you will be tempted to gradually increase your sitting time. However, five minutes is a good minimum for now. If you have your own daily meditation practice, by all means continue practicing as you've been—but I still recommend that you read through the following instructions, just in case you find this way of meditating easier. If you haven't been consistent, it's a sign that your current practice may not be easy enough, and you may want to consider following these instructions instead.

MEDITATION INSTRUCTIONS

Recommended Equipment:

✓ A timepiece that you can see clearly
✓ Comfortable back support

Get comfortable. At some point in the morning, ideally before food or coffee, sit against your headboard while in bed, on a chair, on a couch, in your car, or anywhere with comfortable back support. It's best not to lie down, but it's not necessary to sit up completely straight. "Comfortable" is the key word. Relax your hands and feet, and position yourself as though you were about to watch television. Feel free to rest your legs on an ottoman, or place your feet on the floor. You may also cross your legs or arms if you find it more relaxing.

Position your clock. I recommend using a digital clock app on your phone to track the time, because the LCD display can be easily seen if you're in a dimly lit room. Place your phone in airplane mode and disable the "auto-lock" feature within the app so you won't need to press or swipe the screen in order to see the time. Put the timing device where you can see it clearly without straining, turning your head, or moving your body.

Calculate your finish time. Looking at the clock, add ten minutes on top of your start time. This will be your finish time. So if you begin at 7:30am, your finish time will be 7:40am. Repeat your finish time to yourself once or twice. It's best not to set an alarm, or you may end up shocking yourself out of your meditation.

Close your eyes and relax your body. While your eyes are closed, notice your toes, give them a little wiggle, and relax them. Move your awareness up to your calf muscles, and relax those. Then, move up to your quads, your buttocks, your lower back, your stomach. As one body part relaxes, move up to the next higher part. Relax your hands, arms, shoulders, upper back and chest, throat, lips and tongue, eyes, ears, and forehead. If a part of your body doesn't stay relaxed, that's fine.

Notice your breathing and embrace thoughts. Without speeding up or slowing down your breathing, just notice it. Expect your mind to wander away from noticing your breath. Do not fight this; it's a natural occurrence. It's okay to get lost in thoughts. And whenever you realize you're meditating, just passively begin to notice your breathing again. For now, let the act of meditating become synonymous with both noticing your breathing *and* getting lost in your thoughts. Let all of the thoughts come and go—as you forget and become aware that you are meditating, it's best not to resist any thoughts, including ideas, songs, conversations, images, feelings, or sensations. Embrace all mental experiences without concern, remorse, or regret. In a typical meditation, you'll begin by noticing your breathing for a minute or two, then you'll get lost in thoughts for a minute or two, then you'll remember you're meditating, and slowly return to noticing your breath for a little while, then you'll get lost again.

Check the time. Whenever you have the inclination to look at the time, peek at the clock and verify how much longer you have left, then slowly close your eyes. If only a couple of minutes have passed, return to noticing your breath without controlling it whatsoever. Remember, it's best not to use an alarm or a timer.

Come out slowly and write down your experiences. When you verify that your ten minutes have been reached, your meditation is done. If you want to sit for longer, you can. Otherwise, you may slowly open your eyes and bring yourself out. Once you've completed your meditation, flip to the end of this chapter and briefly jot down your experiences in your inner exercise log. Write a few words about what you felt during your meditation, after your meditation, or any interesting thoughts, ideas, or sensations you may have experienced as a result of your meditation. You can also note the differences in your mood before and after meditating.

Rate your happiness. The "post-meditation happiness level" chart is for you to use to keep track of your progress. Your happiness level should ideally reflect your overall feeling over the previous 24 hours. It's normal for happiness levels to drop at first. As with weight lifting for the first time, there is usually soreness and tightness in the muscles. In your case, there may be some moodiness coming up as a result of meditation. This is a common symptom of purification (we'll dive deeper into that subject in Phase II of The Inner Gym).

ADDITIONAL INSTRUCTIONS

You will meditate each morning, ideally after waking up and before leaving your home. If you miss the morning window, you can make it up later while on your morning commute, at your job, or anywhere else you can find a comfortable seat and close your eyes, including airplanes, buses, and taxis. If you forget to meditate in the morning, just meditate at some point in the afternoon (maybe at your desk), or early evening when you get home. If you would like to meditate a second time in the day or night, feel free to do so.

It's best not to skip meditation if you can help it. It's also recommended to re-read these instructions a few times until you have a full understanding of the simple process. Once you finish this chapter, you're going to stop reading the book and just practice your meditation over the next five days before moving on to the next chapter. You may feel the urge to continue reading, but to get the most out of this program, it's very important that you pace the reading and exercises as instructed.

Helpful tips:

- *You don't have to be a frozen sculpture when meditating. Be natural, and give yourself permission to move, scratch, cough or sneeze during meditation.*

- *If you fall asleep during the meditation, don't fight it off—let it come by lying down if you can.*

- *If you're afraid of over-meditating and missing an appointment, you may use a soft alarm.*

- *If you get distracted, you don't have to start from the beginning—just pick up where you left off.*

- *It's best not to use earplugs or white noise machines while meditating.*

OUTER GYM EQUIVALENT

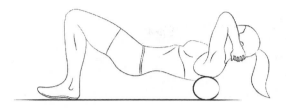

MEDITATING FOR 5 - 10 MINS = FOAM ROLLING

Daily meditation for five to ten minutes is a foundational exercise in your Inner Gym program; just like foam rolling is foundational in the outer gym. Foam rolling should ideally be the first thing you do before working out. By deeply stretching and rolling out your limbs, joints, and muscles, you loosen them for optimal agility. The payoff is superior strength and flexibility once you begin lifting. No serious gym goer skips the foam rolling before working out her outer muscles, and neither should you skip your morning meditation when cultivating your inner muscles.

EXERCISE LOG: MEDITATE 5 – 10 MINS

Day 1

Describe your meditation experiences: _____

_____

_____

_____

Rate my post-meditation happiness level:

Very Happy 10 9 8 7 6 5 4 3 2 1 Very Unhappy

Day 2

Describe your meditation experiences: _____

_____

_____

_____

Rate my post-meditation happiness level:

Very Happy 10 9 8 7 6 5 4 3 2 1 Very Unhappy

Day 3

Describe your meditation experiences: _____

_____

_____

_____

Rate my post-meditation happiness level:

Very Happy 10 9 8 7 6 5 4 3 2 1 Very Unhappy

Day 4

Describe your meditation experiences: _____

_____

_____

_____

Rate my post-meditation happiness level:

Very Happy 10 9 8 7 6 5 4 3 2 1 Very Unhappy

Day 5

Describe your meditation experiences: _____

_____

_____

_____

Rate my post-meditation happiness level:

Very Happy 10 9 8 7 6 5 4 3 2 1 Very Unhappy

Continue on to your next inner exercise after day 5.

He is a wise man who does not grieve
for the things which he has not,
but rejoices for those which he has.

— Epictetus

INNER EXERCISE 2

BE THANKFUL

(Days 6 to 10)

During my first years living in Los Angeles, I made a daily ritual of jogging up Runyon Canyon, a rocky, inclined hiking trail nestled in the Hollywood Hills. My good friend Will joined me on most mornings. Our slow, uphill runs served as strong exercise, as well as opportunities to workshop solutions to everyday work, family, and relationship challenges. Since we were both full-time yoga teachers, many of the resolutions we came up with incorporated Eastern principles, such as being "Self-referral."

Self-referral means looking within yourself to uncover the root of a challenge or complaint—as opposed to being "object-referral," which means to blame a problem on someone else, or external circumstances. For instance, I experienced a decline in modeling jobs during my last couple of years living in New York. I initially blamed it on the economy, but I also knew that I was no longer passionate about being a fashion model. Was my lack of bookings a reflection of the down economy (the object), or my lack of passion (the Self)? Being Self-referral means you give equal consideration to your mindset and actions surrounding a problem as the potential cause of the problem; after all, our thoughts have creative power[vii]. In my case, there were other models who were thriving in the fashion industry, while I was barely scraping by—so it couldn't have solely been the economy.

Another example: let's say someone offends you. If you're being object referral, you automatically blame the offender—they are the problem, not you. But if you're being Self-referral, before assigning blame, you first examine what may be unresolved within you that allowed you to feel offended? Perhaps you've been validating your worth by their opinion of you? Otherwise, why do you care what he or she thinks or says about you? These were the types of conversations Will and I would have day after day.

One morning, something unexpected occurred that lead to the discovery of yet another tool for navigating challenging situations. Will and I were jogging, and I began ranting about how I felt slighted by my ex-girlfriend spreading nasty rumors about me to our mutual friends. I was in the midst of my object-referral tirade, and instead of agreeing that her actions were outlandish, Will interrupted by politely asking me to list off qualities about my ex for which I was grateful.

"Grateful?!" I thought. The last thing in the world I felt in that moment was gratitude. It was like asking me what qualities about neo-Nazism was I most grateful for? Unsure of how to respond to such a bizarre request, I just stopped talking.

At first I was annoyed because he seemed to be taking her side. Next, I remembered our tacit agreement to be Self-referral—but this situation should've been an exception, I thought. Then I slowly began to recognize what he was doing: Will was simply providing me with an opportunity to get out of my "story" of what happened and channel my energy into a more positive direction.

We continued to jog in silence, which amplified the combined sound of heavy breathing and crunching gravel. I strained to play along and began racking my brain for reasons to be grateful. It took about ten more seconds of deep contemplation before I was able to dig something out: "She helped me become more regular in my meditation practice," I whispered, breaking the silence.

Then came another one: "She has one of the most beautiful smiles I've ever seen." After "She's doing the best she can," I was on a roll. And the heavy cloud of negativity, which previously distorted my perception and fueled my rant, began to slowly dissipate. I didn't even realize the grip it had over me until I began mindfully placing my attention on gratitude. Playing this game felt *so* good that I couldn't stop. "She's actually a very caring person." "She's incredibly funny." "I love her family."

I meant every word and instantly felt reinvigorated, both spiritually *and* physically. Then I passed the "gratitude" baton to Will, and he began listing off admirable qualities about his ex-girlfriend, who he'd complained about before as well. Hearing his statements of gratitude inspired me to think of even more of my own. I didn't realize how much my previous wave of negativity was draining my friend's energy and disturbing the serenity of our environment. Afterwards, I felt as bright and expansive as those first morning sunrays emerging from behind us, melting away the shadows of my discontent.

From then on, whenever one of us caught the other tumbling into that very human sinkhole of negativity, we'd break out what became known as the "Gratitude

Game." It was so simple in application, yet immensely powerful in effect.

You can play the Gratitude Game with a friend or by yourself. The trick is to willingly overlook the offender's limitations in favor of his or her admirable qualities. A good starting point is to ask, "What do I admire about this person or appreciate about this situation?" or "What valuable lessons can I learn from this encounter?" If nothing comes, try reverse-engineering the gratitude. In other words, treat the encounter with that person or situation as the best thing that could be happening *for* you in the moment, and work backwards from there by asking yourself why that could potentially be the case? Over time, and with much practice, seeing people's better qualities and feeling a real sense of gratitude becomes habitual.

WHY GRATITUDE?

The opposite of gratitude is resentment. Resentment fosters suffering, and suffering, with no tools to quell it, can feel like quicksand, sucking you deeper into negativity until you're convinced that the world is an awful place. There's no easy (or cheap) way out of this worldview once it swallows you up. This simple inner exercise of expressing daily gratitude will form a taut rope that you can grab a hold of and pull yourself back up to solid ground, where you can see and appreciate all the goodness surrounding you in any moment.

Science has also uncovered several desirable side-effects from experiencing regular doses of gratitude, including the release of very potent "bliss" chemicals.[x] For instance, the pep in my step that I felt while playing the Gratitude Game for the first time, after running uphill and complaining for two miles, was the result of a discharge of the endogenous mood-boosting chemicals serotonin and norepinephrine coursing throughout my body. Studies have also shown gratitude to increase the social bonding hormone oxytocin, and dopamine, which tells the nervous system that the danger is over and it's time to prepare for peace.[xi]

Many of us feel at least a semblance of gratitude before eating, especially on holidays like Thanksgiving. This may seem innate, but feeling grateful before eating is actually a learned behavior—the result of praying or expressing thanks before eating hundreds and thousands of times, after which, seeing a plate of food produces a spontaneous sense of gratitude. But have you ever felt grateful while paying your bills? Or while waiting in line at the post office? The answer is more likely "no" than "yes" because our interpretation of those experiences is that we're losing something—whether time or money—and it's often hardest to feel grateful in the face of loss. But that's about to change.

In these next five days, you're going to stop reserving the feeling of gratitude for meals and start mining for reasons to be grateful when it matters most: during those times when you feel least grateful. We want to build a quick-reflex gratitude muscle that automatically kicks in regardless of whether outward circumstances appear favorable or not. Gratitude is too powerful a feeling with restorative properties for our inner muscles, so we ideally want to experience it as often as possible. It also contains the key to liberating us from our acquisitive-approach-to-happiness mentality, which is the undisputed heavyweight champion of misery.

Like the previous meditation inner exercise, your inner exercise of gratitude will be easy enough to do, no matter how busy you are. It should only take a minute or two each morning. Continue reading for your instructions.

GRATITUDE INSTRUCTIONS

Recommended Equipment:

✓ A writing utensil
✓ An empty jar or container

Assume the attitude of gratitude. Right after your morning meditation, with your eyes still closed, begin to place your attention on a handful of people, places, circumstances, or recent life lessons you're grateful for.

Write five gratitude statements. Slowly open your eyes, grab your book, and in your inner exercise log at the end of this chapter, write down your five statements of gratitude. The following is an example:

What am I grateful for today?
1. My health
2. Having delicious food to eat
3. My job
4. Walks in the park
5. Learning to say 'no'

Keep them with you. After your fifth day you'll begin writing your list on a slip of paper and keeping it with you, ideally in a place where you may stumble upon it hours later, such as in your pocket or purse. It's encouraged that you pull out your list from time to time to reflect on your blessings throughout your day.

Save them. After you fill your exercise log with your gratitude lists, and begin writing them on separate slips of paper, start saving them up. When you get home or at some point near the end of your day, place your list into your "gratitude" jar. The next morning, start again.

Continue listing new statements of gratitude on a daily basis.

Record your happiness. Continue to track your happiness level based on your cumulative feelings over the previous 24 hours.

Helpful tips:

- *It's good to limit your gratitude list to only five statements so you're not racking your brain by the end of the program.*

- *In order to keep this inner exercise easy, it's also recommended to stick with simple statements for each item on your list.*

- *If you forget to write your morning gratitude statements, write it down later, or send it to yourself in an email, or write it in a text message, or say it to yourself and jot it down later. Just make sure you get it into your jar at some point soon. When traveling, keep your daily lists in a safe place and deposit them into your jar when you return home.*

Now you will begin five days of inner gratitude exercises. Resist the urge to start the next chapter until you've completed all five days of writing out your gratitude lists, following your daily meditation practice, which is ongoing.

OUTER GYM EQUIVALENT

EXPRESSING GRATITUDE = HIP OPENERS

Expressing gratitude is like doing a set of hip openers for your happiness. Hip openers are helpful for unlocking tension and negativity stored up from years and decades of stiffness, emotional stubbornness, and inaction. Similarly, this daily gratitude practice will prevent the atrophying of your natural sense of optimism by dissolving negativity that may be stored in your cells. Once your body is free from negativity, it will be far easier to perceive the goodness in every moment. Each time you write your five statements of gratitude, your ability to recognize the beauty surrounding you at all times will strengthen and grow, ultimately becoming impossible to ignore, even on your grumpiest days.

EXERCISE LOG: WRITE 5 STATEMENTS OF GRATITUDE

Day 6

✓ Meditate for five to ten minutes in the morning

What am I grateful for today?

1. _____
2. _____
3. _____
4. _____
5. _____

Rate my post-gratitude happiness level:

Very Happy   10   9   8   7   6   5   4   3   2   1   Very Unhappy

Day 7

✓ Meditate for five to ten minutes in the morning

What am I grateful for today?

1. _____
2. _____
3. _____
4. _____
5. _____

Rate my post-gratitude happiness level:

Very Happy   10   9   8   7   6   5   4   3   2   1   Very Unhappy

Day 8
✓ Meditate for five to ten minutes in the morning

What am I grateful for today?

1. _____
2. _____
3. _____
4. _____
5. _____

Rate my post-gratitude happiness level:

Very Happy   10   9   8   7   6   5   4   3   2   1   Very Unhappy

Day 9
✓ Meditate for five to ten minutes in the morning

What am I grateful for today?

1. _____
2. _____
3. _____
4. _____
5. _____

Rate my post-gratitude happiness level:

Very Happy   10   9   8   7   6   5   4   3   2   1   Very Unhappy

Day 10
✓ Meditate for five to ten minutes in the morning

What am I grateful for today?

1. _____

2. _____

3. _____

4. _____

5. _____

Rate my post-gratitude happiness level:

Very Happy   10   9   8   7   6   5   4   3   2   1   Very Unhappy

Continue on to your next inner exercise only after completing day 10.

*It is one of the most beautiful compensations
of life that no man can sincerely try to help
another without helping himself.*

— Ralph Waldo Emerson

INNER EXERCISE 3

RECEIVE FREELY

(Days 11 to 15)

For about three years in California, my primary mode of transportation was a 2-door Fiat. Here I was, 6'3, 210 lbs, driving a car that was slightly bigger than a matchbox. My friends teased me about it, and I must admit, there were occasions when zipping around Los Angeles in the "Ultimate Parking Machine," as I liked to call it, felt a bit like I was borrowing my girlfriend's car.

This feeling was accentuated one Saturday afternoon when I pulled into a coin-operated car wash for an overdue cleaning. While frantically washing and rinsing the exterior of my Fiat before the allotted four minutes of soap and water expired, I noticed a Ferrari easing out of the washing stall next to mine. Although I never cared much for luxury cars, I couldn't help but marvel at the sleek lines, the craftsmanship, and the feral purr of this matte black Ferrari.

The driver was a burly man, obviously no stranger to the gym. He wore designer sweats and appeared well groomed. Even the towels he was using to dry his car were sparkly white and high quality, the kind you might see poolside at the Four Seasons Hotel. Comparing his car to mine, I began to feel a bit emasculated. "What kind of man drives a Fiat?" I asked myself, while drying the windshield with my yellow reusable towel. In the next moment, I wondered, "Wait, if he can afford a car like that, why was he at the coin-operated car wash? Why not have his car detailed somewhere?"

I took out my bottle of tire polish and began spray-shining my little Fiat tires, careful not to rub the polish onto the tires with my yellow towel so it wouldn't get soiled. I then glanced over at the Ferrari's tires. They were dull, and the thought occurred to offer the Ferrari guy my polish to use on his tires, as a gesture of appreciation and admiration for his well-designed luxury car.

"Hey, I *really* love your car," I said, walking towards the Ferrari guy as he was drying his windows. He paused and met my compliment with a friendly smile.

"I was wondering if you wanted to use my tire polish, because it would be a shame for you to take this beautiful car back on the road without sparkling tires."

With a nod, he happily accepted the tire polish, and I was delighted that I could contribute to making his Ferrari even more spectacular. I walked back over to the Ultimate Parking Machine to finish drying it while he sprayed each of his tires and rubbed the polish in with his white towel.

Then the Ferrari guy did something completely unexpected: he grabbed an unused white towel from his trunk, walked over to my car, knelt down, and began rubbing the polish into my tires. I stood there dumbstruck. Watching this brawny man leave his quarter of a million dollar car to come rub polish into the tires on my tiny eighteen thousand dollar car was such an odd sight. My first instinct was to stop him. I mean, surely he had better things to do than to shine up my Fiat tires. Instead, I decided to receive his kind

gesture, and thanked him profusely for helping me. He
thanked me for offering him the tire polish in the first
place, and began to share his story. He came to the
United States as an immigrant with nothing, and worked
his way up from drying cars at a carwash to becoming
the owner of a Ferrari dealership. He told me he used to
own a Fiat back in Europe. Then he started asking me
about how it drove. "Probably nothing like your
Ferrari," I chuckled to myself.

For about ten minutes, we chatted about all kinds of
things: cars, meditation, and even deeper subjects like
the importance of finding your life's purpose and the
fragility of existence. In the end, he extended an
invitation for me to teach his wife and his staff
meditation. Then we parted ways.

I couldn't help but wonder what would've happened
had I stopped him from rubbing the polish into my tires.
Maybe he would've felt indebted to me, or perhaps we
both would've gone about our day and forgotten about
it. I knew that if I had stopped him, I would've missed
out on a wonderfully inspiring interaction, in which I
got to feel good by helping someone, and he got to
reciprocate. As a result, we both seemed to leave the car
wash in brighter spirits.

There's a place where this kind of unconditional
receiving is expected: Burning Man. It is a festival that
takes place in Black Rock Desert in northern Nevada
every summer just before Labor Day. It's billed as an
experimental community, where art, radical self-
expression and self-reliance are heralded. Attendees
regularly boast that Burning Man is a place where
anything can happen at any time. This is largely due to
Burning Man's "gifting" culture. During the festival,
there is no money exchanged, with the small exception
of coffee and ice. Anything else you receive from
another participant or "camp" must be gifted

unconditionally. In fact, one of the popular to-do's when preparing to attend Burning Man is to plan what you will gift to the other participants.

In a place where unconditional giving is so prevalent, you are sure to find one of the most radical cultures of receiving. Many participants have reported that nowhere else on Earth is the principle of reciprocity and the circulation of resources being demonstrated so thoroughly. "It's not unusual," I heard from someone who attended, "to be standing in the middle of an art installation, contemplating how wonderful it would be to have ice cream—and then seconds later to have a stranger ride up on a bicycle and hand you an ice cream cone, and then disappear into the desert."

Burning Man takes place for only one week out of the year. But could it be possible to create that same level of unconditional reciprocity in daily life? That's what we'll be exploring in this next inner exercise. In anticipation of any skepticism you may have concerning this idea, that receiving ultimately leads to sustained happiness, let's be clear about what we're referring to. There are unconditional gifts, which are offered from the heart, and there are conditional gifts, which are expectation-laden loans disguised as gifts.

Unconditional gifts have no strings attached. They are usually accompanied by an innate feeling of compassion, generosity and spontaneity that is not only detectable, but contagious. It reinforces the beauty of the interdependence of humans when we participate in shared experiences. On the other hand, loans masking as gifts are usually pre-meditated, and accompanied by a detectable underlying expectation for repayment. These gifts detract authentic interaction and activate our defense mechanisms.

Your intuition will tell you which is which. This is why it's important to continue dusting off the body's internal "receiving sensors" through daily meditation. More than anything else, daily meditation will assist you in distinguishing between conditional and unconditional giving. Otherwise, you may accidentally reject what you should have openly received, or vice versa.

For instance, I will never forget when my grandfather, in his final days, called me over one afternoon and offered me one of his fine writing pens. I was 18, and not mature enough to appreciate the appeal of having a keepsake from my grandfather that I could one day pass down to my grandson. Instead, I politely declined his gift. My naïve rationale was that I didn't want the responsibility of caring for his important pen for the rest of my life. He died shortly after. Now, twenty years later, I would give anything to be able to go back and graciously receive his pen. I failed to realize at the time how receiving the pen was more for him than it was for me. The quiet disappointment I saw in his eyes when I rejected his gift still lingers in my memory when I think about my grandfather.

WHY RECEIVING?

In the car wash example, the Ferrari guy's help was unconditional, as was mine. He knew I was capable of shining my tires and I knew he was more than capable of purchasing his own tire dressing. But we were both following an internal, spontaneous prompt to graciously receive—emphasis on *spontaneous*. Unconditional gifts are for the giver. Reception completes the circulation of resources.

To illustrate how receiving works, imagine that buckets of water are being passed down a line from one person to the next, in a group effort to douse a fire. When the bucket gets to you, you don't see it as your possession. Instead, you are the caretaker of that bucket for the brief time it is in your hands, and your job is to accept it, pass it along, and then reach back for the next bucket. This is the essence of circulation. In other words, we are stewards, not the owners, of our resources, whatever they may happen to be. Our job is to receive graciously and care for whatever we've received until the time and inclination comes for us to pass it along to help the next person.

The more you can adopt this attitude towards *everything* you have, the more freely you will experience the flow of abundance. This is true even with our first gift, the gift of life. The following is an excerpt from a speech given by Swami Brahmananda Saraswati, one of the famous Indian Shankaracharyas (King of the Yogis) in the 1940s regarding the gift of life:[xii]

> *To get a human body is a rare thing; make use of it. There are four million kinds of lives which a soul can gather. After that, one gets a chance to be human, to get a human body. Therefore, one should not waste this chance.*
>
> *Every second in human life is very valuable. If you don't value this, then you will have nothing in hand, and you will weep in the end.*
>
> *Because you are human, God has given you power to think and decide what is good and bad. Therefore, you can do the best possible action.*
>
> *You should never consider yourself as weak or a fallen creature. Whatever may have happened up to now may be because you didn't know, but now be careful. After getting a human body, if you don't reach God, then you have sold a diamond at the price of spinach.*

As Swami Brahmananda Saraswati's quote implies, a gift doesn't have to be material. Therefore, we have ample opportunities to practice mindful receiving in just about every aspect our lives. Each morning, we get another day of life, another sunrise, another sunset, another moonlit night, another chance to correct mistakes. As we listen, we may hear the birds sing or leaves blowing in the wind, or we may smell the flowers with their sweet aroma as we pass by them. People may smile at us. These are all precious gifts.

I once witnessed a tailor charge a woman $40 for altering a garment, and then hand her $40 that he found in the pocket of her garment. It was a gift to see something like that—a wonderful reminder of the many good-natured people in the world who go out of their way to do the right thing. Consciously recognizing the gifts bestowed upon us throughout our days will undoubtedly lighten our mood and enhance our interaction with others. The ripple effects of these actions are incalculable.

To take the idea of receiving in another direction, think back to the many moments when it was difficult to appreciate someone for giving you constructive criticism about your job, or about meeting your stated goals more efficiently. If you're like me, at times, you grew defensive, and you didn't express much gratitude. Or you responded with sarcasm, or silence, or by saying something that indicated you were anything *but* grateful. With practice, those moments of feeling rejected will hopefully become fewer and farther in between.

During these next five days, your inner exercise will be to respond by saying "thank you," both in person and through writing. Additionally, you're going to show appreciation for the giver's time, effort, and good intentions. This is a corrective exercise that may expose some weaknesses in your inner receiving muscle. But don't fret, with practice comes supreme strength, and with a brawny receiving muscle, you can never be denied true happiness.

RECEIVING INSTRUCTIONS

<u>Recommended Equipment:</u>

- ✓ Five blank thank you cards or writing paper
- ✓ Five envelopes
- ✓ Five postage stamps (optional)

Be more thankful. Over the next five days, in addition to your five- to ten-minute morning meditation and listing your five statements of gratitude, you will exercise mindfulness of what you're receiving by silently or verbally offering thanks to the people, animals, or nature you encounter for sharing with you their abundance. You won't need to express thanks in any elaborate or subservient way. Sincerely thanking a friend or a stranger (or Mother Nature) for gifting something to you is enough. Communicating how much you appreciate the gift or help goes a long way. Use your best judgment to determine the number of thank you's or the appropriate situations in which you thank someone. Here are some examples of mindful receiving:

- Thanking your spouse for cleaning up behind you
- Thanking the barista for making your coffee
- Thanking someone who offered constructive criticism
- Thanking the chef for the tasty lunch
- Thanking security officers for keeping you safe
- Thanking gardeners, painters, and maintenance crews
- Thanking the cop for your speeding ticket

Choose one person to offer written thanks. Along with oral thanks, you're also going to handwrite either a brief thank you note or thank you card on each day of this exercise to someone who knowingly or unknowingly helped you. For this task, think back to the last time a friend or relative cooked for you or for your family, or went out of their way to help you. Don't forget about your mentors, the doorman, your bus driver, the kid's nanny or schoolteacher, the postal worker. Surely some of these people deserve a little extra recognition for helping you or your family. Now, choose at least one person a day during these next five days and send them a personal, handwritten note or card thanking them. Let them know why you appreciate their gift, service, or presence and how it has helped you.

Record your findings. In your exercise log at the end of this chapter, take a few moments to jot down a short list of five people to whom it would be relatively easy to send thank you cards—people you work with, neighbors, relatives whose addresses you already have (you can modify as you go along)—and have fun exercising the often-neglected receiving muscle.

MORE ABOUT WRITING YOUR THANK YOU NOTES

Few people handwrite and mail letters anymore. You can make someone's day with this small act of kindness and gratitude, while simultaneously training yourself to stay more aware of the gifts in your life. It's a win-win. People love receiving handwritten notes. When is the last time you received a handwritten note from someone thanking you for something you did? How did you feel when you read it? I'll bet it brightened your day.

Regarding style, expressing thanks in your own voice always comes across as more sincere and endearing, so write from your heart.

If you don't have someone's address, choose people who live or work in places you frequent, and you can hand-deliver the notes, drop them in their mailboxes or inboxes, or ask someone to deliver them for you. It's nicer if you add the element of surprise by letting them discover your note as opposed to you giving it to them directly.

Here's an example of a simple thank-you note a man wrote after an overnight stay at his friend's home:[xiii]

Dear Fred,

> *Thanks for putting me up for the night. I know it was an imposition, and I appreciate the special effort you made to provide me with all the comforts of home. I'll give you a call as soon as I get home.*

> *Later,*

> *Mike*

Each time you deliver your card or leave a note, put a checkmark next to that person's name in your inner exercise log at the end of the chapter. After these first five days, you'll continue this habit of either writing a thank you card, leaving a personal handwritten note, or sending a thank you text to someone new every day. This inner receiving exercise will lay the foundation for the upcoming "giving" inner exercise, not to mention it will make you the most appreciative person in the room, which comes with its own rewards.

OUTER GYM EQUIVALENT

RECEIVING FREELY = JUMPING ROPE

Practicing receiving is the equivalent of the jump rope exercise. The two dynamic movements—swinging the rope and jumping high enough for the rope to sweep under your feet—have to be in sync in order for the exercise to work effectively. Likewise, receiving completes the cycle of giving and fosters progressive movement and creation. To stop receiving is to stop jumping, and this can only ever lead to stagnation. Therefore, remember to embrace receiving, which will generate abundance for both you and the giver. Coupled with foam rolling and hip opening stretches, your inner receiving exercise is going to prep you for some heavier lifting down the road!

EXERCISE LOG: RECEIVE FREELY

Day 11

✓ Meditated for five to ten minutes

✓ Listed my five statements of gratitude

Today, I wrote a thank you note to:

_____

Rate my post-receiving happiness level:

Very Happy   10   9   8   7   6   5   4   3   2   1   Very Unhappy

Day 12

✓ Meditated for five to ten minutes

✓ Listed my five statements of gratitude

Today, I wrote a thank you note to:

_____

Rate my post-receiving happiness level:

Very Happy   10   9   8   7   6   5   4   3   2   1   Very Unhappy

Day 13

✓ Meditated for five to ten minutes

✓ Listed my five statements of gratitude

Today, I wrote a thank you note to:

_____

Rate my post-receiving happiness level:

Very Happy   10   9   8   7   6   5   4   3   2   1   Very Unhappy

Day 14

✓ Meditated for five to ten minutes

✓ Listed my five statements of gratitude

Today, I wrote a thank you note to:

_____

Rate my post-receiving happiness level:

Very Happy   10   9   8   7   6   5   4   3   2   1   Very Unhappy

Day 15

✓ Meditated for five to ten minutes

✓ Listed my five statements of gratitude

Today, I wrote a thank you note to:

_____

Rate my post-receiving happiness level:

Very Happy   10   9   8   7   6   5   4   3   2   1   Very Unhappy

Continue on to your next inner exercise after day 15.

The present moment is filled with joy and happiness.
If you are attentive, you will see it.

— Thích Nhất Hạnh

INNER EXERCISE 4

SLOW DOWN

(Days 16 to 20)

One chilly January morning in 2007, Washington, D.C.'s L'Enfant Plaza subway station buzzed with activity. Hurried commuters zipped around the promenade, talking on phones, texting, buying lottery tickets, and lining up to get coffee. Standing in the midst of the hustle and bustle was a lone street performer—a musician—who strummed his violin with unusual passion and dexterity.

The young man was dressed plainly, in a long-sleeved shirt, jeans, and a Washington Nationals baseball cap. Although he performed with the flair of a seasoned entertainer, very few people took notice. The tunnel-visioned commuters continued racing in and out of the station, some with headphones, others yelling into their phones as they darted past the musician.

Despite all of the violinist's theatrics, it took three full minutes before anyone even bothered to look his way. A middle-aged man glanced at the musician for a second or two before shooting off. A half-minute later, the violinist received his first donation from a woman who tossed a dollar bill into the crimson lining of his violin case, which was sprawled out in front of his sneakers. But she, too, rushed along without actually stopping.

It took about six minutes before anyone paused for long enough to listen to a few bars: a businessman, wrapped warmly in a scarf and gloves, leaned against the wall for a few seconds, then glanced down at his watch and left.

After ten minutes, a boy of about three years appeared captivated by the music. He and his mother began a tug-of-war, with his mother finally pulling hard enough and they left—but the boy continued turning his head to glance back. Notably, several other children repeated this action. And every parent, without exception, forced his or her child to move on.

After forty-five minutes of continuous playing, only about seven out of more than a thousand people stopped to listen, and about twenty folks tossed various amounts of pocket change into the musician's case.

The performance ended as quietly as it began. There was no applause. The five or six people lined up at the lottery ticket machine easily outnumbered the maximum amount of people taking notice of the musician at any point during his performance. He humbly packed up his violin, and counted out the $32.15 he received in change and bills, which would normally be a fine amount for less than an hour's work. But this was no ordinary subway performer.

The violinist was a former child prodigy named Joshua Bell—one of the most gifted classical musicians in the U.S. That morning he performed his most enchanting selections, using a 17th-century handcrafted violin worth more than three and a half million dollars.

A few days prior to his incognito subway performance, Bell played before a sold-out crowd in Boston's Symphony Hall for his usual rate of a thousand dollars per minute. Decent seats went for a hundred dollars each. Unbeknownst to almost everyone rushing in and out of L'Enfant Metro Station that morning, an internationally acclaimed musical virtuoso was treating them to a free performance.

Had you or I been walking by Joshua Bell that morning on our way to work, do you imagine that we would've stopped to listen? Of course, there's no way to know, but statistically the answer is a flat no.

Washington Post journalist Gene Weingarten conducted this social experiment to measure people's perception, taste, and priorities. His April 2007 article, "Pearls Before Breakfast," raised some interesting questions—questions we will explore during this next inner exercise. In a commonplace environment, at an inappropriate hour, are we capable of perceiving beauty? And if so, will we take the time to appreciate it? Additionally, if we don't have a moment to stop and listen to one of the most talented musicians in the world playing some of the finest music ever written on one of the most expensive instruments ever crafted, what else are we racing past?

WHY SLOW DOWN?

The feeling of rushing or being hurried is a daily pressure that we have all experienced. Yet not all rushing is a result of being under attack or running late. There's a subtler form of rushing that's more of a subconscious behavior we inherited from our upbringing. For years, we were encouraged to speed through life in an effort to accomplish a series of goals such as learning how to walk and talk, getting potty trained, and making the dean's list.

Once we understood that growing older meant having more freedom, we began hurrying ourselves into the world of cars, relationships, money, and other indulgences. Being an adult also comes with tremendous pressure to make something of our lives. This may entail launching a company, finding a life partner, having kids, or buying a house—and all of this needs to happen within the socially agreed upon amount of time, or we feel like we're behind. The immense pressure to gain acceptance can easily accelerate our lives to an unsustainable pace, where we begin to miss the simpler beauties and joys of being alive.

By the time we approach middle age, the indoctrination to rush is so deeply ingrained that we're prone to become depressed or feel inadequate if we don't accomplish our life goals in time. We may find ourselves obsessing over whether we're heading in the right direction or worrying about what's going to happen to us in the future. Simultaneously, we feel trapped in a never-ending competition for more money, more resources and more love. Our saving grace is the belief that as soon as we get our lives back on track, accomplish our goals, or find our calling, we will fit in and attain ultimate happiness. But it's been pointed out several times already, there is no *way* to happiness, and future happiness should not be the sole motivation for achieving goals.

While no one is immune to this programming, you can slowly override it by exercising the proper inner muscles. Without strengthening these muscles, our acquisitive-approach-to-happiness indoctrination will remain on autopilot, and cause us to overlook the richness and beauty of each moment, where the very happiness we're seeking is hiding in plain sight.

Looking for happiness in future acquisitions is like frantically searching for your phone only to realize moments later you're talking on it. This has certainly happened to me, and how silly did I feel when I realized that I was holding the phone against my ear the entire time while anxiously tearing my place apart looking for it?

The drive to find happiness through achievements strongly influences many of our everyday choices. As a result, we give preferential treatment to the future and see the present as an obstacle we need to overcome in order to reach "success." We justify rushing through our meals, through work, through conversations, and even rushing through relationships in our never-ending quest to reach the next goal. We talk more than we listen and often feel bored whenever we're alone.

In addition to daily meditation, gratitude, and receiving, we need to practice slowing down. Slowing down is a vital component for helping us reconnect to our human experience. It also initiates a refreshing shift away from the old hurry-up-and-get-to-the-future paradigm where, instead of seeking out experiences to make us happy, we seek out experiences that are the perfect outlet for the happiness we have inside. This way, happiness becomes the driving force *behind* the fulfillment of our desires, not the elusive goal.

A good start for approaching this new paradigm is to expect resistance from the subconscious mind, the ego, and society. Remember this: people who spend their lives looking for happiness externally tend to be more object-referral, and therefore they can only ever give you advice corresponding to that worldview. Your ego will also be there rushing you along, trying to convince you that you don't have time to study the clouds, or gaze at the setting sun, or sit by a tree and just gather your thoughts. The ego will tell you there's nothing useful or productive in communing with nature or children, that you must check your phone every minute or see what your social media followers are up to. Expect this voice, and you're better equipped to redirect your attention to the present moment.

It gets easier. Whenever you feel happier and more rested inside (a major byproduct of your daily meditation practice), it's far easier to disregard that voice telling you to hurry and achieve in order to become happier. Conversely, when you're feeling anxious, disregarding that voice is like trying to ignore a shrieking jet engine. Therefore, you must continue to give your meditation the highest priority in order to reduce anxiety, heighten your intuition, rest the body and overcome your conditioning.

Slowing down may also require prompting. You may need to tease your awareness into the present moment and away from the future. Think of it like a pop quiz you'll be giving to yourself on a regular basis. Whenever you feel yourself rushing, obsessing over the future, or getting bored, just ask, "Where is the beauty right now?" See what you can detect. Perhaps you can feel something subtle around you? Or smell something? Or hear something? Maybe there's a valuable life lesson you're learning? Or you realize you're simply more aware of your surroundings nowadays than ever before? How does that make you feel? These questions will reward you with stronger inner guidance.

My meditation teacher used to warn us not to expect mangoes to fall from the apple tree. That was his way of encouraging us to examine our expectations whenever we experience suffering. Perhaps you were expecting the situation (apple tree) to produce a certain outcome (mangoes) that could never occur. When we pay close attention to the present, and particularly to nature, we begin to see what's unfolding more clearly and we learn infinitely more about ourselves and the world around us.

Many ancient stories from Eastern spiritual traditions portray their heroes communing with nature.[xiv] Lessons are often imparted after colorful exchanges with flora, fauna and wildlife. A character may spend significant time walking through the jungle, sitting along the riverbank, or speaking with birds, and receive nuggets of wisdom from nature itself. If you live near a riverbank, or an old wise-looking tree, spend some time sitting next to it and see if you don't receive a deeper sense of your connection to nature, or perhaps more sustainable solutions to the problems you may be facing.

We also don't want to discount experiences of chaos or despair, as a means of receiving valuable insight. The following revelation from the wonderful Hermann Hesse novel *Siddhartha* illustrates this point:

> "*I have had to experience so much stupidity, so many vices, so much error, so much nausea, disillusionment and sorrow, just in order to become a child again and begin anew. I had to experience despair, I had to sink to the greatest mental depths, to thoughts of suicide, in order to experience grace.*"

As you make a sincere effort to slow down, you may begin to recognize that the infinite beauty, connectedness, and love you seek is largely a byproduct of the preceding misery.

While visiting Rome at the turn of the twentieth century, the famous German poet Rainer Maria Rilke wrote to his mentee that though the city was dirty, noisy, and overrun with tourists, "there's still much beauty here, because there's much beauty everywhere." What if we adopted Rilke's outlook more often, no matter where we find ourselves? We can acknowledge the facts of the moment ("The city is dirty, noisy and overrun with tourists") *and* appreciate the goodness ("There's still much beauty here...").

As we stop scarfing down our meals, racing to and from work, speeding through our chores, and ignoring the countless cashiers, waiters, taxi cab drivers, and other human beings we cross paths with every day, an interesting result is sure to follow: we will uncover our own world of exceptional beauty. And we will notice life's little inspirations without trying—those oft-overlooked moments full of insight into our connection with everything and everyone.

Slowing down also has its more obvious benefits. Nutritionists have found that digestion improves when we eat food slowly.[xv] According to cognitive neuroscientists, reading slower enhances our rate of retention.[xvi] Yoga, with its combination of slow stretching and deep breathing, is recognized as one of the most sustainable and beneficial forms of physical exercise. Relationships that evolve slowly tend to last longer.[xvii] In today's information age, knowledge may come fast, but we gain wisdom much more slowly. Do you remember how much you didn't know about the ways of the world five, ten, twenty years ago?

Beauty and happiness are everywhere. The only question is: to what extent can we slow down and be present enough to extract the nectar from each moment? What if normal, everyday life is jam-packed with "Joshua Bell" moments, each with the power to inspire us, enlighten us, or teach us how to live and love better? How many of them can we see? What nuggets of wisdom can we derive from paying closer attention to our surroundings?

During these next five days, you'll move through life as if there are *no* throwaway moments and see how much beauty you can uncover in otherwise ordinary or mundane environments.

INSTRUCTIONS FOR SLOWING DOWN

Select two activities. Pick at least two activities each day that you would normally rush through, and mindfully practice slowing down. Here are some ideas of where to start:

- Getting ready for work
- Showering
- Making a meal
- Chewing your food
- Driving to work
- Doing household chores
- Writing
- Working out
- Walking
- Having a conversation
- Reading the paper
- Performing work tasks

Record them in your log. Feel free to choose more than two activities a day, but make two your minimum. Each morning, after your five- to ten-minute meditation, jot down your statements of gratitude, thank someone for helping you in the past and, in your exercise log, write down the activities in which you will practice slowing down.

Practice slowing down. Once you've listed your activities, practice slowing down while going through them. Maybe try eating slower by putting the fork down in between bites. In conversations, make a point to speak less and listen more. Purposefully leave for work a little earlier in order to take the scenic route. In meditation, go the full ten minutes instead of five—that sort of thing. At the end of the day put a checkmark next to the activities you remembered to slow down with and note any discoveries you made. As an example, it could read:

Day 16:

Today, I practiced slowing down with:

Activity: _Morning meditation_

Activity: _Commuting to my office_

Discoveries: _I felt more connected to others throughout my day and a stronger sense of purpose_

With a little pre-planning, this activity should easily integrate into your daily affairs. Just make sure you allocate enough time to slow down in at least two specified activities. And remember, you're doing this for yourself, to improve your life and increase your happiness. So let the slowing down exercise be organic as opposed to mechanical. Keep your form correct (no cheating!) by immersing your attention completely into the chosen activity. Notice as many sensations as you can.

Practice slowing down for five days before continuing to the next chapter.

OUTER GYM EQUIVALENT

SLOWING DOWN = SHOULDER PRESSES

Each time you successfully slow down, imagine that you've done a mighty set of shoulder presses. The shoulder press is your first inner exercise that equates to weight training, so you should expect it to be difficult, particularly if you go too heavy too quickly. Though it may be difficult, remember that it is a step on an active path towards happiness. Because you've spent the last couple of weeks building up your inner foundation with meditation and mindfulness, and your core with gratitude and receiving, you are conditioned to exercise slowing down with force! As the shoulders bulk up from the shoulder press, they frame the chest in such a way that gives the appearance of supreme strength. Likewise, slowing down and appreciating the moment when you'd rather be rushing gives you internal strength and orderliness. It may seem slight at first, but this muscle builds quickly.

EXERCISE LOG: SLOW DOWN

Day 16

✓ Meditated for five to ten minutes

✓ Listed my five statements of gratitude

✓ Communicated a special thanks to: _____

Today, I practiced slowing down with:

Activity _____

Activity _____

Discoveries:_____

_____

Rate my post-slowing down happiness level:

Very Happy   10   9   8   7   6   5   4   3   2   1   Very Unhappy

Day 17

✓ Meditated for five to ten minutes

✓ Listed my five statements of gratitude

✓ Communicated a special thanks to: _____

Today, I practiced slowing down with:

Activity _____

Activity _____

Discoveries:_____

_____

Rate my post-slowing down happiness level:

Very Happy   10   9   8   7   6   5   4   3   2   1   Very Unhappy

Day 18

✓ Meditated for five to ten minutes
✓ Listed my five statements of gratitude
✓ Communicated a special thanks to: _____

Today, I practiced slowing down with:

Activity _____

Activity _____

Discoveries:_____

_____

Rate my post-slowing down happiness level:

Very Happy   10   9   8   7   6   5   4   3   2   1   Very Unhappy

Day 19

✓ Meditated for five to ten minutes
✓ Listed my five statements of gratitude
✓ Communicated a special thanks to: _____

Today, I practiced slowing down with:

Activity _____

Activity _____

Discoveries:_____

_____

Rate my post-slowing down happiness level:

Very Happy   10   9   8   7   6   5   4   3   2   1   Very Unhappy

Day 20

✓ Meditated for five to ten minutes

✓ Listed my five statements of gratitude

✓ Communicated a special thanks to: _____

Today, I practiced slowing down with:

Activity _____

Activity _____

Discoveries:_____

_____

Rate my post-slowing down happiness level:

Very Happy   10   9   8   7   6   5   4   3   2   1   Very Unhappy

Continue on to your next inner exercise after day 20.

Use this page for additional notes:

If you're important, people will wait.

— Chili Palmer in *Get Shorty*

Inner Exercise 5

BE PATIENT

(Days 21 to 25)

When I taught yoga in the early 2000s, I prided myself on my punctuality. It bothered me when yoga teachers started or finished their classes late. I felt it made them look sloppy and disrespectful of people's time. If you're a teacher and you show up late, you send the message that it's okay for everyone else to arrive late. Plus, you look unreliable and people won't take you seriously.

Fortunately, I lived close to the studio where I taught most of my classes, and had my commute timed down to the minute. It took no more than five minutes to gather my gear and drive to the studio, three minutes to park, and five minutes to get up to the yoga room and set up. If I left 15 minutes early, I would have a few minutes left over to chat with my regulars before the class started.

Out of the hundreds of times I made that commute, one morning stands out. I drove up to the main street leading toward the studio and was surprised to find bumper-to-bumper traffic as far as I could see. I immediately turned around and zigzagged down to the other street heading in the same direction, only to get stuck in even more congested traffic. The odd thing about it was these weren't busy streets, especially not at that hour—and definitely not at the same time. Something highly abnormal was happening.

My heart rate spiked and I became flushed with anxiety. Feeling choiceless and claustrophobic, I sat there like everyone else, inching at a snail's pace toward impending lateness.

I attempted deep yogic breathing, which helped ease my nerves a bit, and from a calmer state, I remembered to call the studio and ask my students not to leave. About ten minutes later, I was nearing the only major intersection of the commute, which would've been the logical site for this mysterious hold-up. Scrutinizing all directions, I saw no obvious cause for the traffic jam. There was no construction, no accident, no ambulance or police tape, nothing unusual whatsoever. And once I got beyond the intersection, traffic began to spontaneously clear up. Now I was even more frustrated because there wasn't even a legitimate reason I could blame for my lateness—I was just plain late.

I parked and bolted up the stairs, now fifteen minutes behind for my class. Then I slowed my pace to a casual walk so I didn't appear rushed in front of my yoga students. That's when I noticed through the glass wall that all of my students were huddled near the back of the yoga room while two janitors were sweeping something up in the front.

As I entered, I felt crunching under my flip-flops. My eyes grew wide as I saw a thousand shards of broken mirror blanketing the floor in the front of the room. Missing from the center-front wall was one of the large mirrored panels. According to the yoga students, the gigantic mirror dislodged and crashed onto the floor about ten minutes before I arrived, which would've been just after my class was scheduled to start. Astonishingly, it shattered in the exact place where I would've been sitting! But because I was late, no one was set up around me to practice yoga and no one got hurt.

The amazing coincidence gave me chills. The random, mysterious traffic jam with no clear cause that I was silently cursing and freaking out about fifteen minutes earlier was actually *saving* my students and I from having a very unlucky start to our day.

I then reflected on a conversation I had about a year prior with a monk at the Hare Krishna temple in Los Angeles. Over lunch, I was telling him about a bad breakup I had recently experienced and how much of an emotional toll it had taken on me. He knew about my commitment to daily meditation and other inner exercises, and responded matter-of-factly by saying, "Good for you. You've been spared."

"How do you mean?" I asked.

"You've got so much spiritual protection around you from all of the inner work you do, that anytime something like that doesn't seem to work out for you, you're just being spared from something much worse."

Needless to say, after the mirror-crashing episode, I truly understood what he was referring to. Ever since then, I've had a much easier time finding patience while stuck in traffic, or in line at the post office. I now know it's likely I'm being protected from something far worse than a mild inconvenience, and the comfort of that understanding allows me to 1) behave like a time billionaire, and 2) stay relaxed when things aren't going the way I would prefer.

The question you're going to explore during these next five days is: what if getting held up in traffic, at airports, in line at the checkout counter, or anywhere inconvenient has the possibility of turning out for good?

And if you hit roadblocks, can you remind yourself to relax, be patient, and treat the "obstacles" as navigational devices towards a better outcome?

WHY PATIENCE?

Patience has always been at the root of slowing down. Now, we're going to give it a little more nuanced attention. While you are still practicing all of your previous Inner Gym exercises, you're now going to include a three-step patience-building exercise that entails:

- Recognizing
- Reorienting
- Remembering

One cause of impatience is a rigid attachment to the outcome or timing of a given situation. Whenever we find ourselves attached to the extent that we can't let go, we make ourselves vulnerable to distress. When we're being impatient, the body initiates a reorganizing of its priorities away from long-term survival functions (like regulating cancer cells, keeping infectious diseases at bay, reproduction, and digestion) toward short-term survival functions (such as the release of coagulants into the bloodstream, increasing the heart rate and level of oxygen consumption, and disabling the part of the brain responsible for rational judgment).[xviii] Therefore, losing patience often can have a dangerously toxic effect on our long-term health. If our goal is to stabilize the feeling of happiness from the inside out, we can't afford to feel impatient too frequently.

PATIENCE INSTRUCTIONS

Here is a detailed explanation of each of the steps you will practice in an effort to remain patient when faced with unexpected change:

Step 1: Recognize. Change is constant. Recognizing that the nature of the world is change and that you have little control over it can help you enthusiastically embrace change when it happens. If and when you find yourself becoming impatient in everyday situations, the opportunity with this step is to recognize that you're more than likely locked onto a specific outcome. For example, during a heated discussion, you may think, "My spouse should be supporting me right now instead of pointing out what's negative about the way I'm debating," or in a traffic jam, you may say to yourself, "There shouldn't be traffic on this stretch of highway at this time of day." These sample thought-patterns stem from a prior attachment to life turning out in a certain way. Recognizing this pattern is your first step in overcoming it.

Step 2: Reorient. French journalist and author Alphonse Karr once wrote, "We can complain because the rose bush has thorns, or we can rejoice because the thorn bush has roses." Once you recognize that an outcome may differ from what you expected or anticipated, you have only a split second to reorient your awareness—or make a better choice about where you place your attention.

If you're quick enough to reorient before the stress response makes you react to the negative aspects (the thorns) rather than reflect on something more positive (the roses), you can effectively neutralize a potentially impatient reaction. Reorienting can take shape in several ways, but at its essence, it means to remove your attention from the offender and place it on something more personally inspiring or positive. The offender may be the negative spouse, the traffic jam, the complaining co-worker, or the tardy friend. Carrie Fisher once said, "Resentment is like drinking poison and waiting for the other person to die." Since you can't control someone else's actions, fighting against them is futile and leads to a more intense stress reaction inside of you, which means that *you* ultimately pay the price. Here are four fast and effective ways to reorient:

Breathe deeply. Take five to ten slow, deep breaths. The stress response causes our breathing to become erratic, and by breathing more deeply we send a message to our body to override the stress response and remain calm and relaxed.

Appreciate the goodness. Take your attention off a potentially negative outcome and place it on whatever good you can derive from the situation (this is a carry-over from your inner slowing-down exercise). Is there a useful message or a valuable lesson you can learn? A favorite Sufi saying of mine is, "If a pickpocket meets a saint, all he sees are pockets." If you train yourself to look for the good in a dilemma, all you will see is the good. Maybe the lesson is that you need to speak up for yourself next time, or that you need to be okay with saying "no" to requests, or that you shouldn't expect apples to fall from mango trees.

Practice thankfulness. Another way you can reorient your attention is by adopting the attitude that while a situation may be far from ideal, it could *always* be worse. A popular Buddhist quote reads, "Let us rise up and be thankful, for if we didn't learn a lot today, at least we learned a little, and if we didn't learn a little, at least we didn't get sick, and if we got sick, at least we didn't die; so, let us all be thankful."[xix]

Survey the surroundings. Many times I've been stuck in traffic or at the dentist's office and noticed something that spawned an idea or a way of thinking that became very useful later on. Nowadays, when life doesn't seem to be going my way and especially if it's out of my hands (which is most of the time), I try to notice what else is taking place around me that I might've otherwise missed. Who are the people around me? Where are they coming from? What art is surrounding me (graffiti, billboards, paintings, hairstyles, fingernails, stylish designs of any kind)? What messages am I detecting? Is there anything relevant for me in this moment? Whenever I step back and look around, I usually see something or someone who inspires me in some way, or that triggers a thought I wouldn't have had if I'd been rigidly fixated on the outcome or timing of the initial situation.

A friend who meditates daily once told me a story about being stuck at O'Hare airport in Chicago during a layover. His connecting flight had already been delayed multiple times. Everyone was growing irritable and frustrated, but he chose to reorient and recognize the opportunity for people watching, one of his favorite pastimes. As he was sitting there watching the travellers, he noticed a familiar face. It was the surgeon who operated on his wife when she lost her battle with cancer a few years before. My friend was so devastated at the time that he never had a chance to properly thank the surgeon for all of his help. He and the surgeon ended up getting coffee together and my friend was able to bring more closure to that chapter of his life. He attributed the patience he felt that day to his regular inner work.

Step 3: Remember. The best indication of what's going to happen in the future is what has happened in the past. In other words, people don't change nearly as fast as we like to think they can or will. Remembering means we pay less attention to what people say and more to what they do. Then remind yourself to make necessary adjustments to your expectations of them based on their actions. If someone is a complainer, remember not to say anything that would trigger his or her complaints. If someone is always late, remember to give him or her a meeting time that's 15 or 20 minutes earlier than you planned to meet. When caught in traffic, remember to take a different route, or leave at a different time, so it no longer feels like a nuisance.

Don't expect people to make adjustments to accommodate your expectations of them. Expecting mangoes to fall from an apple tree only ever leads to more frustration. Instead, loosen your rigid attachment to your feelings of how people should behave. We have very little control of anyone or anything. The more you practice patience, the longer your window of opportunity will be for recognizing, reorienting, and remembering effectively.

Practicing the three "R's" not only leads to more patience, but it also upgrades the quality of your relationships and builds upon your new status as a "time billionaire." Let others rush around in a frenzy while reacting to every little change, demand, or pressure. You will flow through those same changes as gracefully as the Olympic champion swimmer Michael Phelps glides through water. You will also find that acting from patience puts you in the right place at the right time more often than not.

As with your slowing down inner exercise, feel free to choose more ways to practice patience, but give special care to recognizing, reorienting, and remembering. After each day, briefly describe in your exercise log where you practiced the three R's and any valuable takeaways you received from those situations. If you don't find any obvious takeaways, reiterate how you felt by being more patient with yourself and others.

Practice patience for five days before moving on to your final inner exercise. Continue practicing your other inner exercises as well. At this stage, meditating, writing gratitude statements, expressing written thanks, and slowing down most likely require some planning. While it's best not to skip any of those inner exercises, feel free to make them easier by modifying. For instance, instead of writing out your gratitude lists, you may just say the list to yourself at the end of every meditation. And in lieu of sending a thank you card, just shoot off a quick thank you text or email to an unsuspecting friend. Slow down in one activity as opposed to two during these next five days. Meditation is the oil that keeps the other exercises lubricated and propels the engine of inner happiness forward, so remain consistent with that inner exercise.

By the way, you've meditated every day for almost a month now, which is quite an accomplishment. Congratulations on your rock-solid commitment to building happiness within, and continue to track your happiness levels each day you practice patience.

OUTER GYM EQUIVALENT

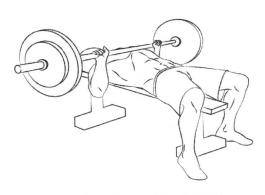

BEING PATIENT = NEGATIVES

Negatives are slow, downward movements of any exercise. They help cultivate the strength it takes to move through the full extension of a particular exercise. For instance, with bench press negatives, you lower the weighted bar down toward your chest very slowly and have your spotter lift the bar back up to your straight-arm starting position. Negatives force you to slow down and feel the weight of the movement, leaving you depleted at the end of each repetition. Ultimately, negatives give you more control and better form when engaging in the full extension of the exercise on your own. Likewise, patience requires you to hold the weight of change longer than you may like, but it also increases your tolerance to the peaks and valleys of future change, strengthening your ability to extend yourself fully in any direction you choose. Each time you practice patience, imagine that you've completed a grueling set of negatives.

EXERCISE LOG: PRACTICE PATIENCE

Day 21

✓ Meditated for five to ten minutes

✓ Listed my five statements of gratitude

✓ Communicated a special thanks to _____

✓ Slow down activity _____

I overcame impatience while: _____

_____

Discoveries: _____

_____

Rate my post-patience happiness level:

Very Happy 10 9 8 7 6 5 4 3 2 1 Very Unhappy

Day 22

✓ Meditated for five to ten minutes

✓ Listed my five statements of gratitude

✓ Communicated a special thanks to _____

✓ Slow down activity _____

I overcame impatience while: _____

_____

Discoveries: _____

_____

Rate my post-patience happiness level:

Very Happy 10 9 8 7 6 5 4 3 2 1 Very Unhappy

Day 23

✓ Meditated for five to ten minutes

✓ Listed my five statements of gratitude

✓ Communicated a special thanks to _____

✓ Slow down activity _____

I overcame impatience while:_____

_____

Discoveries: _____

_____

Rate my post-patience happiness level:

Very Happy   10   9   8   7   6   5   4   3   2   1   Very Unhappy

Day 24

✓ Meditated for five to ten minutes

✓ Listed my five statements of gratitude

✓ Communicated a special thanks to _____

✓ Slow down activity _____

I overcame impatience while:_____

_____

Discoveries: _____

_____

Rate my post-patience happiness level:

Very Happy   10   9   8   7   6   5   4   3   2   1   Very Unhappy

Day 25

✓ Meditated for five to ten minutes

✓ Listed my five statements of gratitude

✓ Communicated a special thanks to _____

✓ Slow down activity _____

I overcame impatience while:_____

_____

Discoveries: _____

_____

Rate my post-inner exercise happiness level:

Very Happy 10 9 8 7 6 5 4 3 2 1 Very Unhappy

Continue on to your next inner exercise after day 25.

*Kindness is the language which
the deaf can hear and the blind can see.*

— Mark Twain

INNER EXERCISE 6

GIVE FREELY

(Days 26 to 30)

Olga, a native of Ukraine, received a full track scholarship from Abilene Christian University, and moved from Eastern Europe to Texas.

When she arrived at ACU, Olga spoke very little English and kept mostly to herself. Whenever she wasn't training, she hid in her dorm room watching television, both as a way to avoid the embarrassment of not yet being able to communicate, and to better understand conversational English. After four years, Olga graduated with her bachelor's degree in fine arts, a handful of track trophies, and the ability to read and speak English fluently.

She moved to Los Angeles, couch-surfed with of some of her former teammates, and spent her days seeking employment as an assistant track coach. But she had a tough time finding work, as few employers wanted the burden of having to file the necessary paperwork to hire her.

I met Olga through mutual friends shortly after her move to Los Angeles and found her humble, curious, and good-humored. I showed her around Los Angeles, taught her meditation, and tried to help in any other way

I could, including treating her to meals and offering to loan her money if she ever needed. Olga probably saw my offers as conditional, seeing as how I didn't hide the fact that I found her attractive. Regardless, she seemed determined to succeed on her own, and my attempts to help were politely declined.

After weeks of scouring the city, Olga finally landed a job as the manager of a high-end sports store in the affluent Brentwood neighborhood. When she told me the good news, I invited her out to lunch to celebrate. Olga said she would love to come, but she needed to be extra-frugal until her first pay check arrived, which meant no wasting gas on non-work-related trips.

After getting off the phone with her, I felt the urge to send Olga some pocket cash, enough for her to get by until her first paycheck arrived. I knew if I asked her or tried to give her money in person, she would continue to refuse. So I got out a pen and paper and began to compose a letter thanking Olga for being such an inspiration by taking a leap of faith, leaving her native culture behind and, without being able to speak English, coming to America to pursue her dreams. I told her how impressed I was by her work ethic and determination.

I then went to the ATM and withdrew $150, which was a fairly substantial amount for me at the time. But deep within, I felt that giving to Olga was no different from giving to myself. I attached a sticky note to the cash, saying that this was an unconditional gift, not a loan, and that I only wanted to help make things easier until her first paycheck arrived. While writing the letter, withdrawing the money, and going to the post office to mail it, I felt an endorphin rush similar to the one I got from jogging.

A few days later, I received a text from Olga thanking me for my gift and saying how the unexpected cash came just in the nick of time. This feeling of helping out a friend in need was delightful, and reward enough for my efforts. Shortly after, Olga began to receive her paychecks, and establish herself as a professional in the American workforce.

Approximately three weeks from the day I mailed Olga the cash, I arrived home from my morning jog and I stopped to grab my mail on my way in. It had been about a week since I last checked it, so the small box was overflowing with the usual mailers, solicitations and bills. As I sorted through the contents, I noticed a thin envelope with a handwritten address buried in between two of the mailers. The letter was from Tamara, an old friend from my modeling days who I hadn't seen or spoken to in months. We both moved from New York to Los Angeles around the same time, and lived not far from one another, but we had fallen out of touch.

One thing about living in southern California's car culture, with its gridlocked traffic and scarce parking, is you can live within a couple of miles of someone and rarely see them. After not speaking with Tam in ages, I was naturally curious to know why she was writing. But I decided not to open her letter immediately. It was so rare for me to receive personal letters that I wanted to cherish it. I gently placed Tam's letter aside and got ready for my day.

After my shower and meditation, I sat down to begin work. I noticed Tam's letter resting on top of my other papers, and decided I couldn't resist any longer. I opened it to find a folded piece of paper, and inside was a personal check for $750. Affixed to the check was a sticky note, which read, "Hey Light, thanks for playing in the Law of Circulation with me." As amazing as it sounds, I had never spoken with Tamara about my theory on circulating resources. But I received her $750 freely, because I was in the habit of giving freely, as I had done with Olga, and understood the importance of keeping the circulation flowing.

When I had my first chance to thank Tam and tell her about the extraordinary coincidence, she revealed to me that one afternoon, out of the blue, she felt a yearning to pull out her checkbook and write me a check. She said the urge was too strong to ignore, and she even described the "high" feeling!

One of the reasons I like recounting this story is because it demonstrates an organic integration of all of the inner exercises at once. There was the expression of gratitude, the receiving exercise, slowing down and showing patience with opening the letter, giving freely, and everyone involved was meditating. The story may seem improbable, but remember that freely circulating your resources can—and will—result in amazing gifts coming to you too. Your inner exercises will make you even more aware of its prevalence.

What you're going to pay special attention to over these next five days are those moments when you have the urge to circulate your resources. You must follow through on that urge without concern, knowing that anything you feel called upon to give from your heart will indeed be returned to you, often in the most unexpected ways, and in far greater amounts than you initially gave.

WHY GIVE?

Do you sometimes feel that you rarely have the desire to give, or that you have the urge, but you don't feel you have enough resources to share—that you're barely scraping by yourself? Or you may feel that you don't really have the urge to give at all. If so, this is a valid observation. Just know that the call to give should feel more internal than external. One of the desirable side effects of daily meditation—another reason why meditation is so important—is that it strengthens the connection between us and everyone else. Surely we can feel traces of a connection without meditation, but meditation makes it more unambiguous and therefore undeniable. That connection will give rise to the feeling you're looking for with this exercise, which is a *spontaneous* urge to give—even during inopportune times.

For instance, you may only have ten dollars to your name, and you feel an impulse to give away five dollars to someone who needs it. Or you're in a hurry to get somewhere, but you feel the urge to stop and help an elderly person cross the street.

The urge to give is less of a passing frivolous desire for indulgence and more of a charming, internal, heartfelt invitation that, in the immediate sense, benefits someone else. The belief governing this circulation of energy states that by giving to others, you give to yourself and by withholding from others, you withhold from yourself.

Giving more is not a question of needing lots of money or stuff to give away, either. You can give a flower. You can offer a silent prayer. You can give a sincere compliment or even just a warm smile. If we feel that we don't have enough material resources to share, just think about how many of history's icons for giving were materially poor—Mother Teresa, Mahatma Mohandas Gandhi, Rev. Martin Luther King Jr., and Jesus, to name a few.[xx] None of these great people were close to having wealth, yet all are synonymous with the spirit of selfless service and giving. King once said, "Everybody can be great. Because anybody can serve. You don't have to have a college degree to serve... You don't have to make your subject and verb agree to serve.

You only need a heart full of grace. A soul generated by love."[xxi]

Understand that both abundance and poverty are states of consciousness. Both influence our perspective on money, time, and resources. One person may see ten dollars as a lot of money that she must save, while another person may view the same amount as pocket change, and spend it without much thought on a short-term craving. Another person may have as their personal mantra "time is money," but may behave in ways that will ultimately lead to poor health, resulting in spending a lot of time trying to recover. Others may act as if they have all the time in the world. Who is ultimately right? Everyone.

Our state of consciousness, whether it reflects abundance or scarcity, is the lens through which we participate in and view our world. People who operate from abundance usually have an easier time seeing and understanding how money and resources *need* to circulate, and how spending actually keeps money in circulation, while hoarding money can lead to unwanted stagnation.

The world's food supply is one example of where a lack of circulation turns an otherwise abundant natural resource into an experience of scarcity. According to *World Hunger: 12 Myths*, the world's farmers produce enough wheat, rice, and other grains to provide every human being with 3500 calories a day.[xxii] That doesn't include many other necessary foods such as beans, nuts, grass-fed meats, fish, vegetables, and fruits. There's more than enough food right now for at least 4.3 pounds of food per person a day worldwide. Yet in many parts of the world, there are food shortages, even starvation. The problem is not lack of supply but a lack of circulation.

Each of us has a unique relationship with the Law of Circulation, and that relationship positively or negatively influences the present degree of abundance we feel in every aspect of our lives. For instance, it may sound counterintuitive to a penny pincher that spending money is good, because lack and limitation have likely become dominant features of their reality. What they don't understand is they've created the reality of scarcity by feeding into it with their reciprocal thoughts and actions. That's why it's good to become extra-mindful of your language around the subject of abundance.

Saying, "I'm broke," or, "I can't afford to buy that," is like dropping a log into the river of abundance. Over time, you will inadvertently construct a dam, blocking your own flow. There is no need to reinforce the reality of scarcity by announcing to the universe repeatedly how much you lack in abundance. And if that's how you truly feel, then you'll be pleasantly surprised with the results of this inner exercise.

Continuing to follow these six foundational inner exercises beyond the initial 30-day program will help you harness abundance wherever you are, and will inspire you to give more easily and freely. With practice, giving your time, attention, or any other resource will feel as easy as giving someone a smile; you won't think twice about it because you'll know the source is limitless, like the sun that offers its light.

The choices we make in every moment dictate the direction of the flow, toward abundance or scarcity, expansion or contraction. Those are our options. Which will we choose? Initially, the easiest choice to make is contraction, because that's our conditioning. We've all heard that it's good to save our money for a rainy day, and that carefree, frivolous spending will lead to the poorhouse. Expect these internal debates to crop up each time you feel the urge to give. To rebut that argument, remind yourself that if spending "wisely" implies getting a substantial return on your investment, then circulating resources is indeed the wisest way to spend.

You begin to know your life is abundant when there's minimal stagnation, hoarding, contraction, or feeling stuck. Your personal fortune may rise or fall many times over, but the feeling inside is that there is always enough.

The inner giving exercise will round out the channels of circulation that we began mindfully practicing earlier. The most important step is to move beyond the intellect, which may ask, "What are you doing?" or "Are you crazy? You can't afford to give that!" and follow your heart, which will highlight the perfect opportunity to give by sending you the signal in the form of an unambiguous urge—one you can't deny—one that will haunt you for days on end if you attempt to ignore it.

Your heart will race with excitement and you will proceed to give, and give openly, generously, and without expectation of receiving anything in return. Your rebate will come from the universe, right when you need it, so there's no need to worry about the timing.

Meditation will play a lead role in this exercise, and as you continue to practice daily, you'll find that several of your most creative ways to give, receive, and express gratitude will show up in your daily meditations or spontaneously throughout your day as a direct result of your meditations.

If you're short on ideas for how to give, take inventory of what you would like to receive. If you want forgiveness, it's a good idea to forgive someone. If you want more love in your life, find ways to give more love. If you want employment, help someone else get a job. If you want to be in a relationship, help someone else find love. Spending your time in service of others is as valuable as spending money, if not more so.

GIVING INSTRUCTIONS

Each day, you will practice giving more of your resources, your smiles, your assistance, your time, and anything else you may have. When someone is speaking to you, give your attention freely. Look them in the eyes. Put away your cell phone. Affirm what they're saying to you. Increasing the quality of your attention will enhance the quality of your interactions with co-workers, friends, partners, your spouse, and children.

During these next five days, tip more than you normally would. Let the waiter, driver, and bellhop know how much you appreciate their service. Maybe even take the time to give feedback to the manager or fill out a comment card offering sincere and lavish praise in those times when you receive exceptional service.

On top of smiling, listening, and tipping well, you're going to give away something that's meaningful to you, and you're going to do it every day. This will allow you to stretch your giving limits quickly and cultivate trust in the understanding that we only ever give to ourselves. Your gift can be in the form of a tithe in church, a donation toward a charitable cause, money for a homeless person, or something that strikes you in the moment. If you feel a slight embarrassment or a financial pinch from the act of giving, then it's a perfect choice. If you feel nothing, then up the ante.

You can also give away your time by volunteering to help someone unrelated to you. It's easy to help our children with homework because that's what we're supposed to do. But helping someone else, especially a stranger, will build your giving muscle quickly. Resources are good to give away as well. Buying a meal for someone in need, offering a ride for an elderly friend or church member, giving your favorite T-shirt to a friend who always comments on how much she loves it, are all strong displays of giving.

There are many obvious and not-so-obvious ways to practice giving. See what you come up with over the next five days and record what you gave each day and to whom. This is a habit you will hopefully continue as often as possible beyond the program.

If the thought of continual giving scares you a bit, it's natural. But there's no need to worry; you won't run out of things to give away, because remember, you'll replenish all that you gave away, plus some. That's how circulation works, and you can now receive these rewards more freely because you're giving freely.

At the end of each day, record what you gave and to whom, and enjoy the rush you get from circulating all of your abundance!

MORE IDEAS FOR EASY WAYS TO GIVE

- Pick flowers from your garden and hand them out to people you visit.
- Anonymously pay for the coffee of the person in line behind you.
- After dining out, give any leftovers to the homeless.
- Make food for the sick and shut-in at your church.
- Volunteer at the local hospice.
- If you notice someone having a difficult day, say a silent prayer for him or her.
- Offer your professional services for free one day.
- Purchase books for the local library.
- If you see trash on the street, pick it up.
- Share your tire polish at the car wash.
- Give hugs.

OUTER GYM EQUIVALENT

RANDOM ACTS OF GIVING = PULL-UPS

A pull-up is one of the most difficult exercises in the gym, because you're lifting your entire body weight. Every pull-up recruits muscles in the entire trunk of your body. The first time you may only perform one repetition, but soon you can do two, then six, and before you know it you're banging out ten full-extension pull-ups. The repetition quickly builds strength in your arms and back, making the once-heavy load feel lighter and easier with time. Your strength in other exercises will also improve. Like pull-ups, the inner exercise of giving uses what you already have to increase strength, and it feels significantly easier with time. In many ways, giving is the centerpiece for sustained levels of happiness just as pull-ups are the measure of a truly in-shape individual.

EXERCISE LOG: GIFT SOMETHING EACH DAY

Day 26

✓ Meditated for five to ten minutes

✓ Listed my five statements of gratitude

✓ Communicated a special thanks to: _____

✓ Slow down activity: _____

✓ I overcame impatience while:_____

Today's gift was: _____

The recipient of my gift was: _____

Rate my post-giving happiness level:

Very Happy 10 9 8 7 6 5 4 3 2 1 Very Unhappy

Day 27

✓ Meditated for five to ten minutes

✓ Listed my five statements of gratitude

✓ Communicated a special thanks to: _____

✓ Slow down activity: _____

✓ I overcame impatience while:_____

Today's gift was: _____

The recipient of my gift was: _____

Rate my post-giving happiness level:

Very Happy 10 9 8 7 6 5 4 3 2 1 Very Unhappy

Day 28

✓ Meditated for five to ten minutes

✓ Listed my five statements of gratitude

✓ Communicated a special thanks to: _____

✓ Slow down activity: _____

✓ I overcame impatience while:_____

Today's gift was: _____

The recipient of my gift was: _____

Rate my post-giving happiness level:

Very Happy 10 9 8 7 6 5 4 3 2 1 Very Unhappy

Day 29

✓ Meditated for five to ten minutes

✓ Listed my five statements of gratitude

✓ Communicated a special thanks to: _____

✓ Slow down activity: _____

✓ I overcame impatience while:_____

Today's gift was: _____

The recipient of my gift was: _____

Rate my post-giving happiness level:

Very Happy 10 9 8 7 6 5 4 3 2 1 Very Unhappy

Day 30

✓ Meditated for five to ten minutes

✓ Listed my five statements of gratitude

✓ Communicated a special thanks to: _____

✓ Slow down activity: _____

✓ I overcame impatience while:_____

Today's gift was: _____

The recipient of my gift was: _____

Rate my post-giving happiness level:

Very Happy 10 9 8 7 6 5 4 3 2 1 Very Unhappy

*Congratulations! This concludes Phase I
of your Inner Gym workout program.
Proceed to your cool down.*

"Everybody wants to get big, but don't nobody want to lift no heavy-ass weights."

— Ronnie Coleman
Eight time winner of Mr. Olympia

COOL DOWN

Congratulations! You made it to the end of the 30-day program, and you've arrived in your new body—your new *inner* body.

Before starting the *The Inner Gym,* perhaps you spent an inordinate amount of time and energy attempting to control your external circumstances in a failed effort to find more increased happiness. Maybe you thought moving locations would do the trick, or breaking up with your partner, or detoxing? And perhaps these changes brought about a temporary wave of joy.

Eventually, we all discover how surprisingly little impact rearranging our external affairs has on our internal state of happiness over the long term—that is, compared to the results of our daily inner work. The outside can never be anything other than a reflection of the strength or weakness of our inner state.

Inner exercising is a practice-oriented practice. The more practice you have, the easier it gets, and the more obvious it becomes that your inner exercises are boosting your baseline level of happiness. Therefore, your inner exercises should remain a non-negotiable priority in your life, along with eating and sleeping, the two activities we all make time for every day.

Of course, this is only the beginning. In addition to feeling happier for no reason, you may notice significant improvements in the following areas:

✓ Less outward neediness
✓ More fearlessness
✓ A greater appreciation for what you have
✓ Less complaining
✓ More connection to your true Self

BE CONSISTENT

Experts say it usually takes around twenty-one to thirty straight days of engaging in a new activity before it becomes habitual. Therefore, I recommend that you continue with all six inner exercises for at least another month. As you practice them repeatedly, they will become permanent fixtures in your daily routine. After a few months, they will remain an integral part of your daily affairs, and you won't have to think about them much at all—which is the point.

True happiness is a state of awareness that doesn't require thinking or planning. If you have to consciously choose to be happy, you're not actually happy. With this workout, you no longer have to play mental tricks on yourself to feign happiness. You now have the mechanics to solidify a foundation of genuine happiness that, once established, isn't going anywhere.

In the meantime, it's important to expect life to catch up to your Inner Gym exercises. You're busy, and you may imagine one day that you don't have time to hit the inner gym, but you mustn't believe it. If you're feeling lazy, remember the small time investment it takes to workout is only ten to twenty minutes of your day. That's doable, even for people with the busiest lifestyles, even for you. Just decide that you have the time and make it a non-negotiable priority.

Gandhi once said, "I have so much to accomplish today that I must meditate for two hours instead of one." Feeling as though there isn't enough time to strengthen your happiness muscles is an indication of inner weakness. It's so tempting to prioritize future goals and achievements over your inner exercises. Much of it stems from the old conviction that future goals and desires are the "yellow brick road" to happiness. As you've experienced in your program, they are not, and your inner exercises will help to keep you anchored in the present moment, where you can continue to create a future that is rooted in the happiness you cultivate today.

As with the outer gym, progress may feel incremental, and it may take a few months before you begin seeing significant results. If you want to stay in top form, you never graduate from needing to exercise. Working out is a strategy, not a tactic. Likewise, strengthening your inner muscles is an ongoing commitment, with eternal rewards. Your workouts have already begun helping you burn your inner fat—that is, rigid attachments to unsustainable or undesirable aspects of yourself. You are now actively engaged in building strong inner muscles, which will yield more confidence, fearlessness, empathy and a higher sense of purpose.

For now, you may continue practicing these six exercises until they are fully ingrained into your daily routine, or if you feel ready to proceed to the next phase, you can find *The Inner Gym, Phase 2: Bulking Exercises*, on theinnergym.com, where you can begin six new inner exercises over the next 30 days. The new inner exercises will help you continue to fortify your happiness and build on the foundation you've established with your first six inner exercises.

Otherwise, stay the course, stay inspired, and I wish you the very best in your Inner Gym workouts. Congratulations again for having completed this first phase of the program and thank you for being a part of this movement.

Please share your experiences with The Inner Gym community at theinnergym.com or on our Facebook page: facebook.com/theinnergym.

i Helliwell, John F., Richard Layard, and Jeffrey Sachs, eds. "World Happiness Report 2013." New York: UN Sustainable Development Solutions Network. 2013. p. 39.

ii Helliwell, John F., Richard Layard, and Jeffrey Sachs, eds. "World Happiness Report 2013." New York: UN Sustainable Development Solutions Network. 2013. Figure 2.6: Comparing Happiness: 2005–07 and 2010–12 (Part 3), p. 29.

iii Taylor, Jill Bolte. "My Stroke of Insight: A Brain Scientist's Personal Journey." New York, Viking, 2008. p. 183.

iv Basta, Maria , M.D., and George P Chrousos, M.D., and Antonio Vela-Bueno, M.D., and Alexandros N Vgontzas, M.D. "Chronic Insomnia and Stress System." Sleep Med Clinic. June 2007, pp. 279–291.

v Journal of Clinical Psychology "A meta-analysis of 146 independent studies found that the Transcendental Meditation technique is twice as effective at reducing trait anxiety when compared with concentration, contemplation or other techniques." Stanford University.1989. pp. 957–974.

vi Puff, Robert, Ph.D. "Meditation Will Make You Smarter (And Happier)." Meditation for Modern Life. September 15, 2013.

vii Atasoy, Ozgun. "Your Thoughts Can Release Abilities beyond Normal Limits." Scientific American. August 13, 2013.

x Leone, Shakaya. "Gratitude: The Secret Beauty Elixir." Aspire Magazine. 2011.

xi Algoe, Sara B., and Baldwin M. Way. "Evidence For A Role Of The Oxytocin System, Indexed By Genetic Variation In CD38, In The Social Bonding Effects Of Expressed Gratitude." Social Cognitive Affective Neuroscience, 2014.

xii "Rocks Are Melting: The Everyday Teachings of Swami Brahmananda Saraswati. Jagadguru Shankaracharya and Jyotir Math," 1941-53.

xiii Leas, Connie. "The Art of Thank You." MJF Books. 2002. p. 80.

xiv Long, Charles H., and George Braziller. "Alpha: The Myths of Creation." n.p. 1963.

xv Kokkinos, Alexander, and Carel W. le Roux 1, and Kleopatra Alexiadou, and Nicholas Tentolouris, and Royce P. Vincent, and Despoina Kyriaki, and Despoina Perrea, and Mohammad A. Ghatei, and Stephen R. Bloom, and Nicholas Katsilambros. "Eating Slowly Increases The Postprandial Response Of The Anorexigenic Gut Hormones, Peptide YY And Glucagon-Like Peptide-1." 2010 Jan; 95(1):333-7. doi: 10.1210/jc. 2009-1018. Epub 2009 Oct 29.

xvi Radach, Ralph, and Alan Kennedy, and Keith Rayner, eds. "Eye Movements and Information Processing During Reading." European Journal of Cognitive Psychology, 2004, p. 16.

xvii Sassler, S., Addo, F. R., & Lichter, D. T. "The tempo Of Sexual Activity And Later Relationship Quality." Journal Of Marriage And Family. 74. 2012. pp. 708-725.

xviii Oxford Brookes University, "Stress Management." n.p. n.d. https://www.brookes.ac.uk/student/services/health/stress.html

xix Buscaglia, Leo. "Born for Love: Reflections on Loving." n.p. 1992.

xx Marques, Joan F. "On Impassioned Leadership: A Comparison Between, Leaders From Divergent Walks Of Life." International Journal of Leadership Studies. 2007. pp. 98-125

xxi King, Martin Luther, Jr. "Drum Major Instinct." An adaptation of the 1952 homily ''Drum-Major Instincts,'' by J. Wallace Hamilton. February 4, 1968, xxii Lappe, Frances Moore, and Joseph Collins, and Peter Rosset with Luis Esparza. "World Hunger: 12 Myths." 2nd edition. New York. Grove Press. 1998.

Made in the USA
Lexington, KY
07 August 2017